1981

The Year You Were Born

Compiled by

JEANNE MARTINET

Illustrated by

JUDY LANFREDI

Tambourine Books New York

U.S. Almanac
1981

World population 4,500,000,000

United States population 229,807,000
Males 111,876,000
Females 117,931,000
People over age 65 25,500,000

Number of births in the U.S. 3,629,000
Boys 1,860,000
Girls 1,769,000
Average weight at birth 7 pounds, 7 ounces

Deaths in the U.S. 1,978,000

Size of the U.S. 3,618,770 square miles

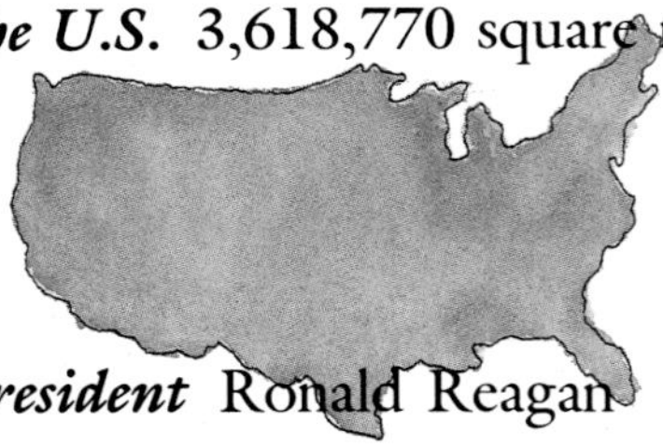

President Ronald Reagan

Biggest state (in area)
Alaska, 591,004 square miles

Longest river
Mississippi-Missouri, 3,710 miles

Tornadoes
783

Percent of households with TV sets
98%

Percent of households with VCRs
1.8%

1981
The Year You Were Born

Birth Certificate

Name: ______________________

Birthdate: ______________________

Time: ______________________

Place of Birth: ______________________

Weight: ____________ Length: ________

Mother's maiden name: ______________

Father's name: ______________________

To my parents, Mudzo and Dather J.M.

For my dear friend Sherree J.L.

Inquiries should be addressed to Tambourine Books, a division of William Morrow & Company, Inc., 1350 Avenue of the Americas, New York, New York 10019.
Printed in the United States of America

ISBN 0-688-12875-0 (pbk.) ISBN 0-688-12874-2 (lib. bdg.)

1 3 5 7 9 10 8 6 4 2
First edition

Number of telephones in the U.S.
150,000,000

Top crop
Corn, 208,000,000 metric tons

Children's books sold
123,000,000

Boy Scouts 3,244,000
Girl Scouts 2,276,000

Most popular girl's name Jennifer
Most popular boy's name Michael

Top dog
Poodle, 93,050 (registered)

Most rain
Mobile, Alabama, 57.12 inches

Most snow
Marquette, Michigan, 221.6 inches

New patents (inventions)
65,000

Top spectator sport
Horse racing, which drew 75,463,000 fans

Motion picture attendance
1,067,000,000

Pieces of mail handled by the U.S. Postal Service
110,130,000,000

Bald eagles living in the U.S.
13,709

January

*J*anuary is named after Janus, the Roman god of doorways and of beginnings.

BIRTHSTONE *Garnet*

THURSDAY
January 1

New Year's Day • Greece officially becomes the 10th member of Europe's Common Market. • In Paris, France, workers begin renovating the Eiffel Tower.

FRIDAY
January 2

Eileen Anderson takes office as the mayor of Honolulu; she's the first woman to run this city since 1893 when Queen Liliuokalani was overthrown.

SATURDAY
January 3

On this day in 1959, Alaska became the 49th state of the Union. • In 1847, a small town in California called Yerba Buena was renamed San Francisco.

SUNDAY
January 4

Scientists in Switzerland report the world's first cloning of a mammal. Cells from mouse embryos (fertilized eggs) have been used to create 3 new mice.

MONDAY
January 5

President-elect Ronald Reagan meets with President José López Portillo of Mexico to try to strengthen the friendship between the 2 countries. • Steam rises from Mount St. Helens volcano in Washington.

TUESDAY
January 6

A dog named Reno is rescued in southern Italy after being buried for 48 days by an earthquake!

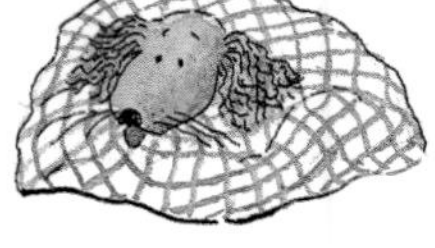

WEDNESDAY
January 7

A Canadian archaeologist has found Stone Age cave art in the British Isles. The rock carvings, which are of 2 bison and an unknown animal, were made before 13,000 B.C. and are the first of their kind to be found in this part of the world.

THURSDAY
January 8

Power failure in Utah and in parts of Idaho and Wyoming. 1,500,000 people are without electricity for 6 hours. • A flu epidemic sweeps the U.S.

FUN FACT '81

11 billion video games are played every year.

STAR QUEST

WHO ELSE WAS BORN IN JANUARY?

ALBERT SCHWEITZER

German physician, philosopher, missionary, musician
Albert Schweitzer dedicated his life to helping people and animals; in 1913, he founded a hospital in French Equatorial Africa (now Gabon). He won the 1952 Nobel Peace Prize.
BORN January 14, 1875, in Kaysersberg, Germany (now France)

FRIDAY
January 9
In Japan, the world's only performing giant panda, Wei Wei, attacks 2 of his handlers from the Shanghai Circus, biting them both in the foot.

SATURDAY
January 10
A collector in Palm Beach, Florida, buys the Brasher doubloon—one of the world's most famous coins—from Yale University for $650,000.

SUNDAY
January 11
The longest and fastest crossing of Antarctica is completed by a 3-man British team from the Trans-Globe Expedition. They have traveled 2,600 miles, passing through the South Pole, in only 66 days.

MONDAY
January 12
Terrorists called the Macheteros blow up 11 U.S. military jet fighters at the Muñiz Air National Guard Base near San Juan, Puerto Rico. The bombs totally destroy 9 of the planes and cause $45,000,000 in damage.

TUESDAY
January 13
In Tunisia, it snows for the first time in 25 years!

WEDNESDAY
January 14
Freezing weather has damaged the fruit and vegetable crops in Florida. In some parts of the state, the temperature is at a record low of 8°F.

THURSDAY
January 15
Martin Luther King, Jr.'s Birthday • A candy maker in Oakland, California, ships 32,000,000 red, white, and blue jelly beans, Ronald Reagan's favorite candy, to Washington, D.C., for the upcoming inaugural celebration.

FRIDAY
January 16
Rex Wood lands a world record 348-pound, 5-ounce southern bluefin tuna off the coast of New Zealand.

SATURDAY
January 17

At Leech Lake in Minnesota, the International Eelpout Festival's eelpout fishing contest begins. • President Ferdinand Marcos of the Philippines ends the state of martial law that has been in effect there for 8 years, 4 months.

SUNDAY
January 18

ICE-SCAPING? 3 youths who are stranded on a piece of floating ice in the Hudson River are rescued by helicopter. As soon as they reach shore, they are arrested for purse-snatching!

MONDAY
January 19

Astronomers at the University of Wisconsin announce the discovery of the largest star ever found. 150,000 light-years away, it is 3,500 times bigger and 10 times hotter than the sun.

TUESDAY
January 20
Full Moon

Ronald Reagan, age 69, is inaugurated as the 40th president of the United States. He is the oldest man ever elected to that office. • 52 American hostages in Iran are freed after 444 days in captivity. They are flown to West Germany in preparation for their return to the U.S.

BIRTHDAYS IN 1981

LOS ANGELES 200 YEARS!
MAYONNAISE 225 YEARS!
PLAYER PIANO 100 YEARS!
CANNED RATTLESNAKE MEAT 50 YEARS!
BULGARIA 1,300 years!
EMPIRE STATE BUILDING 50 YEARS!
WONDER WOMAN 40 YEARS!
BOYS CLUB OF AMERICA 75 YEARS!
BALLET 400 YEARS!
COLOR PHOTOGRAPHY 50 YEARS!
AMERICAN RED CROSS 100 YEARS!
MATCHES 300 YEARS!
THE JOFFREY BALLET 50 YEARS!
ALKA-SELTZER 50 YEARS!
ATOMIC CLOCK 25 YEARS!
SCRABBLE 50 YEARS!

WEDNESDAY
January 21

Mexico and Cuba sign a special pact in which Mexico promises to help solve Cuba's energy problems by training Cubans, supplying equipment, and joining Cuba in exploring for oil and gas.

THURSDAY
January 22

In Oslo, Norway, a 5-nation conference decides that the polar bear should remain a protected species.

FRIDAY
January 23

2 masked men steal $500,000 worth of diamonds from a jewelry merchant's office in New York City.

SATURDAY
January 24

In Poland, millions of workers stay home from their jobs in order to protest; they want a 5-day instead of a 6-day work week. • An elephant named Sonja is stolen from a zoo in Copenhagen, Denmark.

SUNDAY
January 25

The Oakland Raiders beat the Philadelphia Eagles, 27–10, in Super Bowl XV. • In New York City, a man and a woman hijack a helicopter and land it on a prison roof to help an inmate escape. The attempt fails: They can't cut through the wire mesh that covers the roof!

MONDAY
January 26

The U.S. Supreme Court rules that states are now free to allow criminal trials to be televised.

TUESDAY
January 27

Happy birthday, Mozart! • After 20 years of research, an artificial heart for humans is approved by doctors at the University of Utah.

WEDNESDAY
January 28

It's raining colored dust—probably blown from the Sahara Desert—over Scotland and Northern Ireland.

THURSDAY
January 29

Ronald Reagan holds his first press conference as president of the United States.

FRIDAY
January 30

Norway's prime minister resigns. • A ticker tape parade is held in New York City to celebrate the return of the American hostages. 971 tons of confetti greet the 21 hostages who attend.

SATURDAY
January 31

In New York, the Indian Point nuclear power plant is shut down after radioactive leaks are discovered.

CIA AGENT
GETS 15 YEARS
FOR SPYING
FOR KGB

BLIZZARDS
IN THE
MEDITERRANEAN

MAN JUMPS
FROM
EMPIRE
STATE
BUILDING

DROUGHT
EMERGENCY
DECLARED
IN NEW YORK
CITY

February

*T*he name February comes from the Latin *Februa*, which means "feast of purification."

BIRTHSTONE *Amethyst*

SUNDAY
February 1
The U.S. Coast Guard rescues 80 fishermen who have been stranded for several hours on a 5-mile-long piece of ice in Lake Erie. The ice had broken loose from the shore.

MONDAY
February 2
Groundhog Day. Punxsutawney Phil sees his shadow, meaning 6 more weeks of winter! • South Korean president Chun Doo Hwan meets with President Reagan in Washington, D.C.

TUESDAY
February 3
3 divers at Duke University in North Carolina break the deep diving record. In a simulated dive, they survive pressure equal to that found 2,250 feet below sea level. • A dentist in Syracuse, New York, reports that the president's favorite food, jelly beans, is worse for teeth than other candy.

WEDNESDAY
February 4
Gro Harlem Brundtland becomes Norway's first woman prime minister. • A town called Grantham has been voted the most boring place in England.

THURSDAY
February 5
Chinese New Year, the beginning of the Year of the Rooster • In Australia, the world's largest batch of Jell-O—7,700 gallons—is made in a special tank. The Jell-O flavor is pink watermelon!

FRIDAY
February 6
The first 12-screen movie theater in the U.S. opens in Rockaway Township, New Jersey.

FUN FACT '81

An anteater can devour up to 30,000 ants a day and can flick its tongue 160 times in a minute!

SATURDAY
February 7
At the National Inventors Day celebration in Arlington, Virginia, Paul B. MacCready, inventor of human-powered aircraft, is named Inventor of the Year.

SUNDAY
February 8
Dianne North catches a record-breaking thresher shark—weighing an amazing 802 pounds—off the coast of Tutukaka, New Zealand.

1981: CHINESE YEAR OF THE ROOSTER

February 5, 1981–January 24, 1982

Chinese horoscopes follow a 12-year cycle, with each year represented by an animal. According to legend, Buddha summoned all the animals in the world to him one New Year, promising them a reward. Only 12 obeyed, and he gave them each a year. The Rat arrived first, so he got the first year! The order of the cycle is always the same: Rat, Ox, Tiger, Hare, Dragon, Snake, Horse, Sheep, Monkey, Rooster, Dog, and Pig.

Roosters are dreamers, but they know how to speak their minds. They are daring, brave, and self-reliant. Roosters like to be noticed and are good company; they are also very active and work hard. Roosters are usually good at earning money. They get along well with Oxen, Snakes, and Dragons but *not* with Hares or other Roosters.

Some famous roosters: Joan Benoit, Eli Whitney, Grover Cleveland, Goldie Hawn, Hirohito (Japanese emperor)

MONDAY
February 9

The head of Poland, Jozef Pinkowski, is replaced by the Minister of Defense, General Wojciech Jaruzelski.

TUESDAY
February 10

A pug called Ch. Dhandy's Favorite Woodchuck (nicknamed Chucky) wins best-in-show at the Westminster Kennel Club dog show, out of 2,910 dogs. • The biggest storm of the winter sweeps from the Rocky Mountains to the Great Lakes.

WEDNESDAY
February 11

The *Polar Sea* becomes the first ship ever to reach the northernmost place in the U.S.—Point Barrow, Alaska, 300 miles north of the Arctic Circle.

THURSDAY
February 12

Lincoln's birthday • In New York City, 30 men and 8 women compete in a race—up 1,575 steps—to the top of the Empire State Building. Peter Squires wins, with a time of 10 minutes, 59 seconds.

FRIDAY
February 13

A long-lost symphony in F major, composed by Wolfgang Amadeus Mozart when he was 9, has been found in Bavaria.

SATURDAY
February 14

Valentine's Day • The first attempted nonstop round-the-world balloon journey is abandoned when the balloon, the *Jules Verne*, is forced to land in northern India.

SUNDAY
February 15

Richard Petty wins the Daytona 500 automobile race for the 7th time! • A rare bird called the black-tailed godwit is spotted on Merritt Island, Florida.

MONDAY
February 16

A company called United Bio-Fuel Industries has announced its plans to use city garbage to make ethanol. The ethanol can then be used to make gasohol, a type of fuel.

TUESDAY
February 17

The National PTA (Parent-Teacher Association) was founded on this day in 1897.

WEDNESDAY
February 18
Full Moon

A British antique 18-carat-gold watch is sold for $145,000 in New York City, the most anyone has ever paid for a watch in the U.S. Its workings are very complicated; it even chimes!

THURSDAY
February 19

Happy birthday, Copernicus, the Polish astronomer born in 1473. • Susan Brown has been chosen to row in the Oxford-Cambridge boat race in England, breaking a 52-year-old men-only tradition.

INVENTOR OF THE YEAR

Paul B. MacCready, a physicist and an aeronautics expert, is the inventor of the first human-powered aircraft. His most famous inventions are pedal-operated planes—the *Gossamer Condor* and the *Gossamer Albatross*—and the *Solar Challenger*. The *Solar Challenger* is the first aircraft to fly powered only by solar cells and the first solar aircraft to cross the English Channel. MacCready used unusual materials like plastic and piano wire to build the *Solar Challenger*, in order to keep it lightweight.

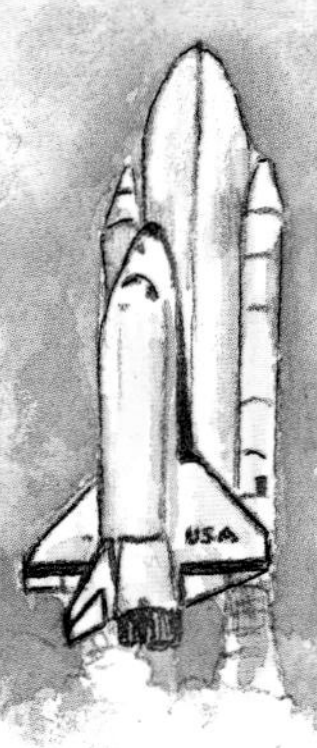
USA

FRIDAY
February 20

At exactly 8:45 A.M., U.S. space shuttle *Columbia* tests its engines at Cape Canaveral in Florida. The test lasts for 20 seconds.

SATURDAY
February 21

The annual Giant Seafood Festival is held in Grant, Florida. • In 1878, the first telephone book was issued, in New Haven, Connecticut.

SUNDAY
February 22

George Washington's birthday • SHEIK THIEF: $1,500,000 worth of jewelry is stolen from the penthouse of Saudi Arabian sheikh Wadji Tahlawi in Miami, Florida.

WHO ELSE WAS BORN IN FEBRUARY?

THOMAS EDISON

U.S. inventor
Often called the world's greatest inventor, Edison invented more than 1,300 things in his lifetime, including the electric light bulb, the phonograph, and an early version of the movie camera. His birthday is celebrated in the U.S. every year as National Inventors Day.

BORN February 11, 1847, in Milan, Ohio

MONDAY
February 23

John Paul II becomes the first pope to visit Japan. • In Miami, Florida, 2 men are caught with the 43 pieces of Sheik Wadji Tahlawi's stolen jewelry in the trunk of their car.

TUESDAY
February 24

ROYAL NEWS FLASH! The engagement between Prince Charles and Lady Diana Spencer is announced in England. The engagement ring is an oval sapphire surrounded by 14 diamonds set in 18-carat white gold.

WEDNESDAY
February 25

Several earthquakes rumble in Athens, Greece. • Bird-watchers from all over the nation have flocked to Merritt Island, Florida, to get a glimpse of the 16-inch black-tailed godwit, first spotted 10 days ago. It is usually seen only in northern Europe, 3,500 miles away.

THURSDAY
February 26

The prime minister of England, Margaret Thatcher, visits President Reagan in the White House. • A long-nosed potoroo, a small, rat-like kangaroo, is born at the London Zoo.

FRIDAY
February 27

A helicopter crashes into the crater of Mount St. Helens in Washington. Good news: The pilot and the 4 scientists aboard are okay!

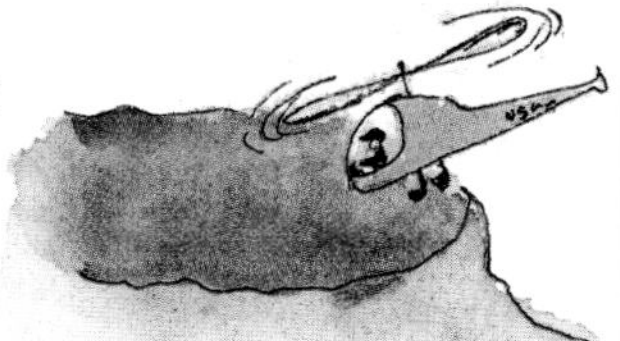

SATURDAY
February 28

HEFTY THEFT: Two 200-pound bronze doors have been mysteriously stolen from a cemetery on Staten Island, New York.

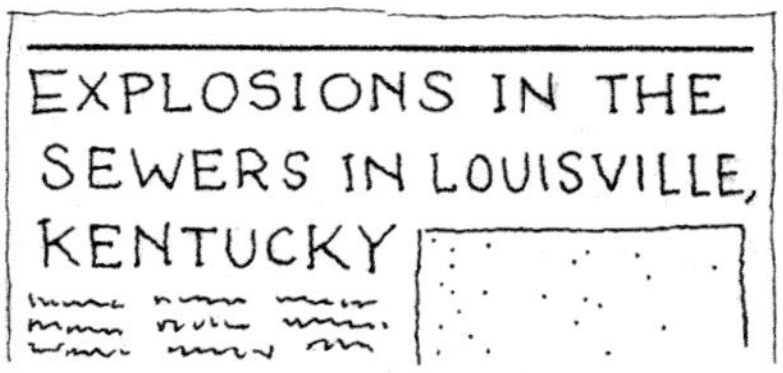
EXPLOSIONS IN THE SEWERS IN LOUISVILLE, KENTUCKY

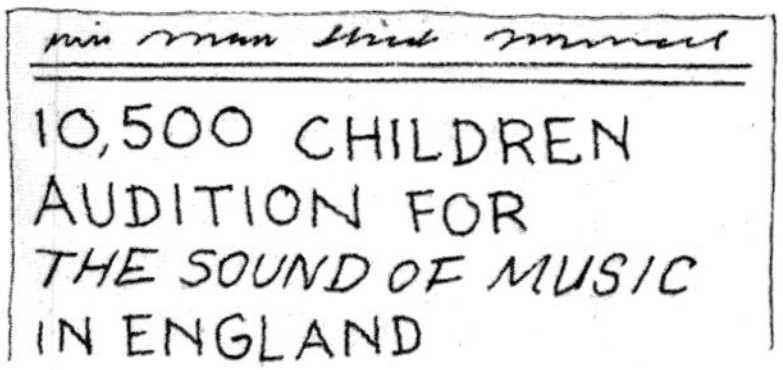
10,500 CHILDREN AUDITION FOR THE SOUND OF MUSIC IN ENGLAND

ITALY'S MOUNT ETNA SPEWS LAVA

March

*M*arch is named for the Roman god of war, Mars.

BIRTHSTONE *Aquamarine*

SUNDAY
March 1
Scientists at the University of California report the sighting of 4 new galaxies about 10 billion light-years away from earth.

MONDAY
March 2
Typhoon Esau strikes American Samoa in the Pacific Ocean, causing major damage. • Dr. Seuss is 77 years old today. 12 states declare it Dr. Seuss Day!

TUESDAY
March 3
Chia Chia, a giant panda, leaves England's London Zoo for the U.S., where it is hoped that he will mate with Ling Ling at the National Zoo in Washington, D.C. (Chia Chia means "the very best"; Ling Ling means "cute little girl.")

WEDNESDAY
March 4
A strong earthquake—measuring 6.3 on the Richter scale—rocks Athens and southern Greece.

THURSDAY
March 5
At the world figure-skating championships in Hartford, Connecticut, Scott Hamilton of Haverford, Pennsylvania, wins in men's singles.

FRIDAY
March 6
Denise Biellman of Switzerland wins the women's world figure-skating championship in Hartford, Connecticut.

FUN FACT '81

Approximately 120,000,000 Girl Scout cookies are sold in the U.S. in 1981.

SATURDAY
March 7
40-year-old Ricardo Hoffman has reached Santa Elena, Argentina, after swimming a record 299 miles in the Paraná River! It took him 84 hours and 37 minutes.

SUNDAY
March 8
More than 100 people compete in the nation's largest crossword puzzle tournament, held in Stamford, Connecticut. Phillip M. Cohen of Alquippa, Pennsylvania, wins first prize.

MONDAY
March 9
Girl Scouts Week • In New York City, 40,000 wristwatches worth $1,560,000 are stolen from a warehouse in Queens.

TUESDAY
March 10

President Reagan visits Canadian prime minister Pierre Elliott Trudeau. • On this day in 1862, the United States issued its first paper money.

WEDNESDAY
March 11

Scientists discover hair grass growing on Refuge Island in Antarctica. It's the southernmost flowering plant ever found. • A U.S. aircraft carrier rescues 17 people from the South China Sea after an Indonesian helicopter crashes.

THURSDAY
March 12

The Soviet Union announces that it has launched a space capsule, the *Soyuz T-4*, carrying 2 cosmonauts. Destination: the *Salyut 6* space station, which is orbiting the earth.

FRIDAY
March 13

The world's largest diamond, the 170.45-carat Star of Peace, is sold for $20,000,000. • A 4-pound gold bar is found in the mud at a building site in Mexico City. It's discovered to be part of the long-lost treasure of the Aztec emperor Montezuma II.

SATURDAY
March 14

IT'S ABOUT TIME: FBI agents have found the 40,000 watches stolen on March 9. They were in a garage on Long Island.

SUNDAY
March 15

Buzzard Day in Hinckley, Ohio • One of the largest butterfly collections in the world has been donated by Arthur C. Allyn, Jr., to the University of Florida in Gainesville. There are 1,500,000 specimens in the collection!

MONDAY
March 16

George F. Kennan wins the Einstein Peace Prize for his efforts to improve relations between the United States and the Soviet Union.

TUESDAY
March 17

St. Patrick's Day • Tracks have been found in the jungles of Borneo, East Malaysia, which show that as many as 10 Sumatran rhinoceroses may still be on the island. They were thought to be extinct there.

WEDNESDAY
March 18

President Reagan declares Louisville, Kentucky, a major disaster area because of damage caused by explosions in the sewers in February.

THURSDAY
March 19

Swallow Day in San Juan Capistrano, California. Every year on this day, the town's swallows return from their winter home 6,000 miles away in Argentina.

FRIDAY
March 20

Full Moon

Spring equinox • Dr. Daniel Shu Jen Choy has invented a new cure for seasickness: the Seasick Strap. It's a piece of elastic that fits around the wrist and puts pressure on acupuncture points.

SATURDAY
March 21

In New York City, thousands of people attend the Superstar Baseball Card Show. Willie Mays signs autographs.

SUNDAY
March 22

Postage for first-class letters goes up from 15 cents to 18 cents. • Soviet spaceship *Soyuz 39* is launched to link up with the orbiting space station *Salyut 6*.

1981 AWARDS BOARD

Nobel Peace Prize: Office of the United Nations High Commissioner for Refugees
National Teacher of the Year: Jay Sommer of New Rochelle, New York
National Spelling Bee Champion: Paige Pipkin, age 13, of El Paso, Texas
Female Athlete of the Year: Tracy Austin, tennis
Male Athlete of the Year: John McEnroe, tennis
Horse of the Year: John Henry
Best Movie (Academy Award): *Chariots of Fire*
Best Special/Visual Effects (Academy Award): *Raiders of the Lost Ark*
Best Album (Grammy Award): John Lennon/Yoko Ono, *Double Fantasy*
Best Single (Grammy Award): Kim Carnes, "Bette Davis Eyes"
Best children's book (Newbery Medal): *Jacob Have I Loved* by Katherine Paterson
Best children's book illustration (Caldecott Medal): *Fables*, written and illustrated by Arnold Lobel

BEST

MONDAY
March 23

In Japan, crowds of people flock to a high-technology fair, Portopia '81, which features dancing robots, computers that compose music, and an 8-mile-long artificial island. There are 32 pavilions and 900 guides.

TUESDAY
March 24

U.S. customs agents seize 614 pounds of Bolivian cocaine worth $217,000,000 from a small plane they followed to Colombia. • The Casio Computer Company announces plans to make a computer small enough to fit inside a person's pocket.

WEDNESDAY
March 25

Space shuttle *Columbia*'s fuel tank, which is 154 feet long, is pumped full of super cold fuel in a special test to make sure the tank's insulation is working. The tank holds 520,000 gallons!

WHO ELSE WAS BORN IN MARCH?

MR. ROGERS (FRED ROGERS)

U.S. educator, TV personality, author
He is the producer and host of the popular children's show "Mister Rogers' Neighborhood." Mr. Rogers has worked in children's television since 1954 and has written many books for young people.

BORN March 20, 1928, in Latrobe, Pennsylvania

THURSDAY
March 26

A man in Montreal, Canada, hijacks an armored truck and gets away with $2,400,000. Guards chase the truck in a taxi but can't catch it.

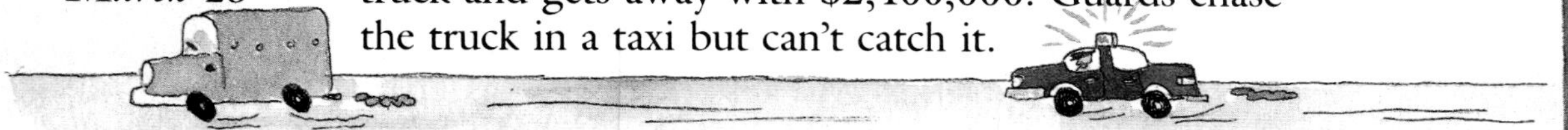

FRIDAY
March 27

A woman from the environmental group Greenpeace chains herself to a Japanese whaling ship off the east coast of Japan. She's protesting the killing of sperm whales, which are in danger of becoming extinct.

SATURDAY
March 28

In Switzerland, Phil Mahre from Yakima, Washington, becomes the first American to win the World Cup skiing title.

SUNDAY
March 29

FAST FRIENDS? At the first London Marathon, the winners cross the finish line hand in hand: Inge Simonsen of Norway and Dick Beardsley of the U.S.

FINISH

MONDAY
March 30

A gunman shoots and wounds President Reagan, his press secretary, and 2 law-enforcement officers as they are walking to the president's limousine in Washington, D.C. • Indiana State beats North Carolina, 63–50, in the NCAA basketball championship.

TUESDAY
March 31

At Bristol University in Great Britain, a 3,000-year-old Egyptian mummy is unwrapped!

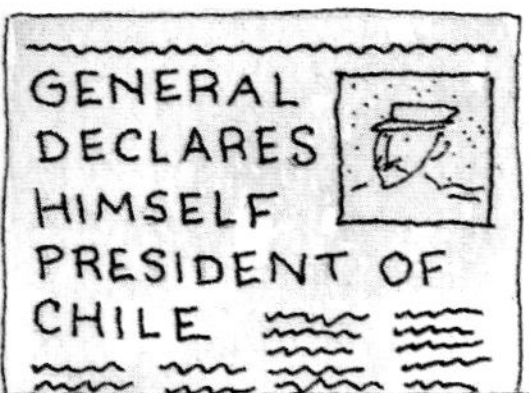
GENERAL DECLARES HIMSELF PRESIDENT OF CHILE

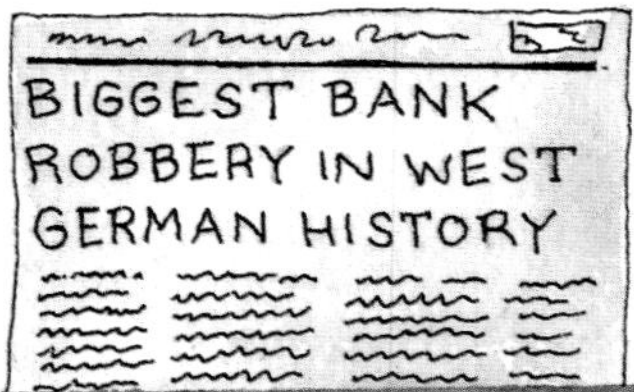
BIGGEST BANK ROBBERY IN WEST GERMAN HISTORY

156,000 HELIUM BALLOONS RELEASED IN JAPAN— BREAKS WORLD RECORD

April

*T*he name April comes from the Latin *aperire*, which means "to open." April is known as the time of budding.

BIRTHSTONE *Diamond*

WEDNESDAY *April 1*
April Fools' Day • President Reagan, who is recovering in the hospital, is moved from intensive care to a private room. He was shot in the chest on March 30.

THURSDAY *April 2*

A tornado in Hurtsboro, Alabama, leaves 300 people homeless. The town only has 800 people!

FRIDAY *April 3*
A forest fire starts in Arkansas. Officials suspect arson.

SATURDAY *April 4*
In Rome, Italy, police capture the leader of the Red Brigade, Mario Moretti.

SUNDAY *April 5*
The 5-day countdown to the launching of the first U.S. space shuttle, *Columbia*, begins.

MONDAY *April 6*
The fire raging in Arkansas is finally brought under control. It has burned 12,000 acres and is the largest forest fire in the state for 10 years.

TUESDAY *April 7*
Chia Chia, the panda visiting from London, meets Ling Ling, the National Zoo's panda, for the first time when their cages are placed side by side today.

WEDNESDAY *April 8*
Inspectors have discovered that 8,000 gallons of radioactive water has leaked from the Indian Point nuclear power plant in New York. Some of it has drained into the Hudson River! The plant has been shut down since January 31.

GONE WITH THE WIND

SAVINGS BOND

On April 4, a violent tornado hits West Bend, Wisconsin, causing about $15,000,000 of damage. Among the belongings that are swept away by the tornado is a $1,000 savings bond owned by Eugene Dunn. Imagine his surprise when someone in Sheboygan Falls, 30 miles away, finds it and returns it to him!

WHO ELSE WAS BORN IN APRIL?

MAYA ANGELOU

U.S. actress, author, poet
Her many books include *I Know Why the Caged Bird Sings* (1970) and *Gather Together in My Name* (1974).
BORN April 4, 1928, in St. Louis, Missouri

THURSDAY
April 9
A U.S. nuclear-powered submarine runs into a Japanese freighter in the East China Sea, and the Japanese ship sinks.

FRIDAY
April 10
Mysterious computer problems delay the liftoff of *Columbia*—just a half hour before launch. • In Washington, Mount St. Helens erupts, shooting steam and ash 15,500 feet above sea level.

SATURDAY
April 11
President Reagan is released from the hospital, only 12 days after being shot in the chest. • Jobless youths riot in London, England.

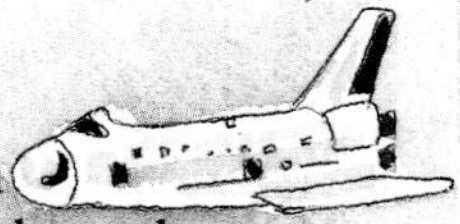

SUNDAY
April 12
At 7:00 A.M., space shuttle *Columbia* takes off from Cape Canaveral, in Florida, for its first test flight. Aboard are astronauts John W. Young and Robert L. Crippen.

MONDAY
April 13
The son and grandson of the famous Russian composer Dimitri Shostakovich have defected from the Soviet Union and are seeking political asylum in West Germany. Maksim Shostakovich, a conductor, and his son, a pianist, are headed for the U.S.

TUESDAY
April 14
Space shuttle *Columbia* lands at Edwards Air Force Base in California after a flight of 54 hours, 22 minutes, and 36 orbits of earth.• Pandas Chia Chia and Ling Ling are finally placed together in a pen at the National Zoo in Washington, D.C., but all they do is hit and shove each other!

WEDNESDAY
April 15
A 25,000-pound sperm whale tries to beach itself at Coney Island, New York. Police lead the whale back out to sea.

THURSDAY
April 16

The sick sperm whale is found again in shallow water at Oak Beach. It has pneumonia! Marine biologists tow it to a place nearby where they can try to nurse it back to health.

FRIDAY
April 17

Good Friday • Robots have been invented that can play chess.

SATURDAY
April 18

17-year-old Boy Scout John Loftus jumps into the Ottauquechee River near Woodstock, Vermont, to save Liz Rocha from drowning. Her homemade raft had flipped over during a race.

SUNDAY
April 19
Full Moon

Easter. Also the first day of Passover. • Wayne Caswell lands a 13-pound, 5-ounce lake whitefish in Meaford, Canada, the biggest of its kind ever caught.

MONDAY
April 20

The 85th Boston Marathon is won by Toshihiko Seko of Japan with a time of 2 hours, 9 minutes, 26 seconds. The women's winner, Allison Roe of New Zealand, finishes in 2 hours, 26 minutes, 45 seconds—a course record.

TUESDAY
April 21

The Soviet Union launches *Cosmos-1266*, an unmanned satellite that will do space research.

$
$

WEDNESDAY
April 22

Earth Day • 5 tornadoes hit eastern Missouri and move through the state and down into Texas. • In Tucson, Arizona, a robber steals $3,300,000 in cash from a bank, one of the largest thefts of its kind in U.S. history.

COLUMBIA

The U.S. space shuttle *Columbia* is the world's first reusable spacecraft. It took 10 years and almost $10 billion to develop. About the size of a DC-9 jet, it is the first spaceship to have wings and a tail. *Columbia* is 122 feet long and weighs 107 tons.

About 1,000,000 spectators watch the launching of the shuttle's first mission on April 12. The roar of the engines is so loud that it scares 2 bald eagles into leaving their nests near Kennedy Space Center. During the 54½-hour mission, *Columbia* completes 36 orbits of the earth before reentering the atmosphere and gliding to a halt on a dry lake bed in the desert in California.

Columbia is built to go up into space 99 more times!

FUN FACT '81

The speed of the Earth in orbit around the Sun is 18.5 miles per second.

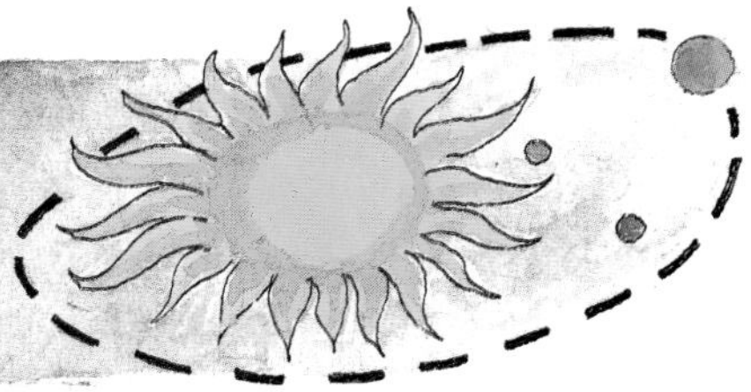

THURSDAY
April 23

Doctors in Boston, Massachusetts, report the development of an artificial skin to replace real skin that has been destroyed by burns. The fake skin is made of cowhide, shark cartilage, and plastic.

FRIDAY
April 24

The federal Centers for Disease Control reports that measles should be completely eliminated by the end of 1982.

SATURDAY
April 25

Physty, the 23-foot-long sperm whale found near Coney Island and nursed back to health by marine biologists, is released into the open sea today, 10 days after he was found. 11 boats and more than 5,000 people cheer him on.

SUNDAY
April 26

ROYAL KLUTZ: Great Britain's Prince Charles falls off his horse during a polo match in Australia. It's the 3d time in 6 weeks that he has fallen from his horse!

MONDAY
April 27

Scientists in Peru have uncovered 7,700-year-old skeletons which may prove that the village of Paloma is the oldest human community in the Americas.

TUESDAY
April 28

President Reagan appears in public today for the first time since he was shot on March 30. He makes a speech to Congress.

WEDNESDAY
April 29

At 8:00 P.M., red and blue laser lights are beamed from the top of the Empire State Building to begin the celebration of its 50th anniversary.

THURSDAY
April 30

Doctors at Harvard University in Cambridge, Massachusetts, report they have created a powder that can make bone grow in humans.

MATTER AND ANTIMATTER COLLIDED FOR FIRST TIME
RECORD PRICE OF $990,000 PAID FOR MEDIEVAL TAPESTRY
KANGAROOS CAUSE HAVOC IN AUSTRALIAN TOWN
PRINCE CHARLES VISITS WASHINGTON, D.C.

May

*M*ay comes from Maia, who was the Roman goddess of growth, increase, and blossoming.

BIRTHSTONE *Emerald*

FRIDAY *May 1* — Happy 50th birthday, Empire State Building! • Today Henry Cisneros takes office as the first Mexican-American mayor of a major U.S. city—San Antonio, Texas.

SATURDAY *May 2* — The Kentucky Derby is won by a horse named Pleasant Colony, ridden by jockey Jorge Velásquez. Pleasant Colony beats Woodchopper by less than a length.

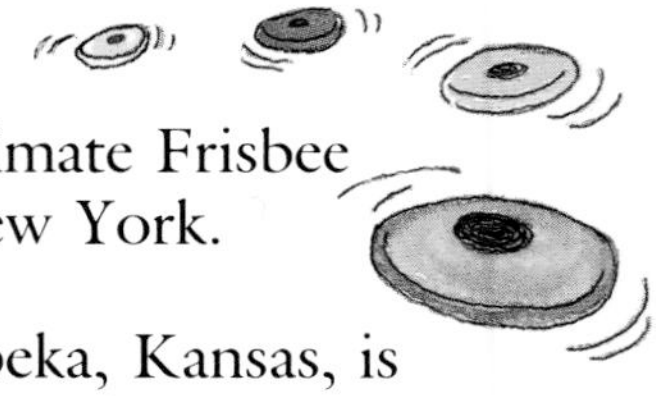

SUNDAY *May 3* — The 5th annual Eastern United States Ultimate Frisbee Championships take place in Purchase, New York.

MONDAY *May 4* — 61-year-old Henrietta Jean Crouch of Topeka, Kansas, is named 1981 Mother of the Year • 9-year-old Girl Scout Markita Andrews of New York City has sold 2,245 boxes of Girl Scout cookies!

TUESDAY *May 5* — To celebrate the 50th anniversary of Great Britain's Royal Ballet, *The Sleeping Beauty* is performed at Covent Garden in London.

WEDNESDAY *May 6* — At 7:19 A.M., a Norwegian freighter collides with a Staten Island ferryboat in thick fog near the Statue of Liberty in New York Harbor.

THURSDAY *May 7* — The FBI has arrested a guard at the Smithsonian Institution and 2 other men for stealing objects from the Washington, D.C., museum—including a 35-inch gold, diamond-studded sword, and a silver pen that was used to sign the Treaty of Paris.

FRIDAY *May 8* — A large, rapidly growing sinkhole appears in Winter Park, Florida.

SATURDAY *May 9* — The sinkhole in Florida swallows up a house, 6 cars, and a camping vehicle. • A blue 5-cent stamp posted in 1846 in Alexandria, Virginia, is sold to a European collector for $1,000,000. The first official U.S. stamp wasn't issued until 1847!

SUNDAY
May 10
Mother's Day • Stunt motorbike rider Ellie Taylor breaks a women's world record by jumping over 5 buses in Northamptonshire in England. She also breaks her nose.

MONDAY
May 11
The sinkhole in Florida, which is more than 1,000 feet wide and 170 feet deep—and still growing—has swallowed a swimming pool!

TUESDAY
May 12
A Polish Expedition sets out to cross the deepest canyon in the world—Cañón de Colca in Peru. It's 10,574 feet deep.

WEDNESDAY
May 13
While riding in an open car in St. Peter's Square at the Vatican in Italy, Pope John Paul II is shot and wounded by an escaped Turkish criminal. • Tornadoes totally flatten 22 buildings in Emberson, Texas.

THURSDAY
May 14
The Boston Celtics win the NBA basketball championship against the Houston Rockets. • The Soviet Union launches the *Soyuz 40* spacecraft to link up with the *Salyut 6* space station. On board: the first Romanian astronaut.

FRIDAY
May 15
For the first time in 26 years, one of the 2 volcanoes on the island of Pagan in the Pacific Ocean erupts, sending ash 40,000 feet in the air and hot lava toward a village.

SATURDAY
May 16
The Preakness is won by Pleasant Colony, the horse that won the Kentucky Derby on May 2. • International Chicken Flying Meet in Columbus, Ohio.

SUNDAY
May 17
Nancy Reagan has been named honorary president of the Girl Scouts.

EMPIRE STATE BUILDING TURNS 50

When the 1,250-foot-high Empire State Building first opened on May 1, 1931, it was the tallest building in the nation. It was designed by William T. Lamb and cost $12,000,000 to build. 10,000,000 bricks were used in the construction. The skyscraper has 102 stories, 6,500 windows, 61 passenger elevators, and 6 freight elevators. In 1945, a B-25 bomber crashed into the 79th floor, killing the crew and 11 people in the building. However, not very much damage was done to the building itself. The Empire State Building has its own fire brigade, its own police force, and even its own post office. Every year there is a race to the top, up the 1,575 steps!

MONDAY
May 18

8 tornadoes destroy houses and barns throughout Kansas and Oklahoma. • The Rocky Mountains in Colorado get 11 inches of snow.

TUESDAY
May 19
Full Moon

Forest fires spread through south Florida. More than 385,000 acres have been blackened since January 1.

WEDNESDAY
May 20

At the St. Louis Zoo in Missouri, 4 Mexican wolf pups are born to the only female Mexican wolf in captivity. The wolves are an endangered species.

THURSDAY
May 21

The New York Islanders beat the Minnesota North Stars to win their 2d straight Stanley Cup in professional ice hockey. • A painting by Pablo Picasso is sold for $5,300,000—the most ever paid for a painting by any 20th-century artist.

CHILDRENS ZOO

FRIDAY
May 22

A riot breaks out at a prison in Jackson, Michigan. • The Children's Zoo at the Bronx Zoo in New York City reopens. It has new exhibits that allow kids to see what it feels like to be a spider, a turtle, or a snail.

SATURDAY
May 23

MORE PRISON TROUBLE: 3 guards at the maximum security prison near Carson, Nevada, are taken hostage by inmates.

SUNDAY
May 24

Bobby Unser, driving a Norton Spirit, wins his 3d Indianapolis 500. Average speed: 139 miles per hour!

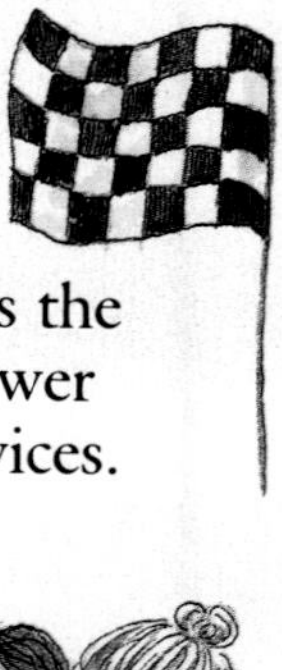

MONDAY
May 25

Memorial Day • A man dressed as Spider-Man climbs the world's tallest building—the 1,454-foot-high Sears Tower in Chicago—using a rope, suction cups, and metal devices. It takes him 7½ hours.

FUN FACT '81

There are 6,000,000 more women than men living in the U.S.

WHO ELSE WAS BORN IN MAY?

MALCOLM X (born MALCOLM LITTLE)

U.S. civil rights leader
He had risen to the top of the Black Muslims by 1963 but formed a new group in 1964, the Organization of Afro-American Unity. The new group stood for brotherhood between the races instead of separation. Malcolm X was assassinated in 1965.

BORN May 19, 1925, in Omaha, Nebraska

TUESDAY
May 26

2 Soviet cosmonauts return to earth in the *Soyuz T-4* after 75 days in space. • At the Southern Michigan Prison in Jackson, Michigan, 1,000 inmates with clubs take over a cell block and set it on fire. The riot, the 2d in 5 days, lasts 9½ hours.

WEDNESDAY
May 27

Willie Shoemaker wins the 8,000th race of his career at Hollywood Park, California. He has won more races than any other jockey.

THURSDAY
May 28

A duck named Donna recuperates after having surgery in Las Vegas, Nevada. She's just had an arrow removed from her breast!

FRIDAY
May 29

The leaders of the United Mine Workers, the coal miners' labor union, end the union's 72-day strike, after reaching a new agreement with employers for better wages and benefits.

SATURDAY
May 30

Donna the duck is back in her pond on a golf course in Las Vegas, Nevada, where she lives. She is given a feast of corn to celebrate her return.

SUNDAY
May 31

Jean Hinckley catches a 38-pound, 8-ounce halibut near Santa Cruz, California. It's the biggest fish of its kind ever caught.

NEW ANIMAL CALLED A UNIGOAT UNVEILED

FRANÇOIS MITTERRAND BECOMES PRESIDENT OF FRANCE

12-YEAR-OLD TO ATTEND NEW YORK UNIVERSITY

USSR DRILLS WORLD'S DEEPEST HOLE

June

*J*une is named for the Latin *juniores*, meaning "youths," or from the goddess Juno.

BIRTHSTONE *Pearl*

MONDAY
June 1
China publishes its first English-language newspaper, based in Peking.

TUESDAY
June 2
President Reagan meets with his press secretary, James Brady, for the first time since they were both shot in March. • 300 inmates of a Hawaii prison take over a cell block.

WEDNESDAY
June 3
A dozen tornadoes touch down in Denver, Colorado.

THURSDAY
June 4
After a high-speed car chase, police in Des Moines, Iowa, catch a man who is charged with stealing $2,000,000 in jewelry. He is also a suspect in the spectacular bank robbery that took place in Tucson, Arizona, on April 22.

FRIDAY
June 5
A rare Siberian crane is born at the International Crane Foundation in Baraboo, Wisconsin. • Carl Lewis wins the NCAA sprint and long jump during competition in Italy.

SATURDAY
June 6
The Belmont Stakes horse race is won by Summing, ridden by jockey George Martens. • The world's first test-tube twins are born in Melbourne, Australia.

SUNDAY
June 7
Israeli planes bomb and destroy an atomic reactor near Baghdad in Iraq. • In tennis, Bjorn Borg wins his 6th French Open championship.

FUN FACT '81

Starfish have an eye at the end of each of their arms. They can also grow back an arm if they lose it!

WHO ELSE WAS BORN IN JUNE?

FRANK LLOYD WRIGHT

U.S. architect
One of the most important architects in U.S. history, he introduced the Prairie style, which used strong horizontal lines and low roofs. He liked to use natural materials. His famous buildings include the Guggenheim Museum in New York City and the Robie House in Chicago, Illinois.
BORN June 8, 1867, in Richland Center, Wisconsin

MONDAY
June 8
President José López Portillo of Mexico meets with President Reagan at the White House. • In Chicago, Illinois, stuntman Daniel Goodwin is fined $35 for climbing the Sears Tower on Memorial Day.

TUESDAY
June 9
On this day in 1902, the first Automat, a restaurant with vending machines, opened in Philadelphia, Pennsylvania.

WEDNESDAY
June 10
MONSTER SIGHTING: The famous Lake Champlain sea monster—nicknamed Champ—is spotted by a fisherman near Grand Isle, Vermont.

THURSDAY
June 11
A major earthquake rocks Kerman Province in Iran, causing a national disaster. It registers 6.8 on the Richter scale.

FRIDAY
June 12
U.S. baseball players go on strike. This is the first time the players have gone on strike in the middle of the season.

SATURDAY
June 13
Officials at the Haight-Ashbury Free Medical Clinic in San Francisco, California, announce that acupuncture—a method of treating illness or pain by sticking very fine needles into certain points in the body—can be used to treat drug addiction.

SUNDAY
June 14
Flag Day • A Polish kayak team completes the crossing of the world's deepest canyon, Cañón de Colca in Peru. They set out on May 12.

MONDAY
June 15

In 1752, Benjamin Franklin, flying a kite during a thunderstorm, proved that lightning is a form of electricity when a bolt hit his kite and nearly killed him.

TUESDAY
June 16

Baseball's Chicago Cubs are sold by William Wrigley to the Tribune Company for $20,500,000.

WEDNESDAY
June 17
Full Moon

GATOR-BREAK: Albert the alligator climbs over a fence at the Denver Zoo in Colorado and escapes!

Heh, heh, heh!

TEETH THIEF

On June 19, a set of George Washington's false teeth are reported missing from a storage room at the National Museum of American History in Washington, D.C. Made in 1795 for President Washington by his dentist, John Greenwood, the dentures are gold and ivory, not wood, as many people believe. The teeth have written on them: "This was the great Washington's teeth." There are at least 3 other sets of Washington's dentures in existence: one at Mount Vernon (his home on the Potomac River); another in London, England; and a third somewhere in South America.

THURSDAY
June 18

The U.S. Department of Agriculture announces that scientists have found a way to use gene-splicing to make a vaccine that fights hoof-and-mouth disease.

FRIDAY
June 19

Superman II opens in 1,395 movie theaters across the U.S. • Western Europe's Ariane rocket is launched from French Guiana and boosts 2 satellites into orbit around the earth.

SATURDAY
June 20

Superman II sets a record for the best single day in movie history when it sells a whopping $5,603,000 in tickets!

SUNDAY
June 21

Father's Day • Summer Solstice • In Bozeman, Montana, Chuck Simonson wins the College National Finals Rodeo men's all-around title, as 5,400 people cheer him on. The women's title is won by Anna Crespin.

MONDAY
June 22

Researchers in Kenya have found evidence that a group of prehistoric humans killed 90 giant baboons about 500,000 years ago at a special butchering ground, apparently in some sort of ritual.

TUESDAY
June 23

In Florida, dolphins are being trained to help divers find sunken treasure!

WEDNESDAY
June 24

Zookeepers in Colorado are still searching for Albert, the alligator that ran away from the Denver Zoo. The keepers are using long poles with nooses attached.

THURSDAY
June 25

The 68th Tour de France bicycle race begins in Nice, France.

FRIDAY
June 26

The Great Muppet Caper, a movie starring Kermit the Frog and Miss Piggy, opens in New York City.

SATURDAY
June 27

Balloons from 22 countries compete in the hot-air balloon championships in Battle Creek, Michigan.

SUNDAY
June 28

Voyager 2, which was launched in 1977, sends back its first photographs of Saturn. • Happy birthday, Arthur Reed of Oakland, California—he's 121 today!

MONDAY
June 29

The U.S. Postal Service issues a special stamp recognizing 1981 as the International Year of the Disabled. • *Superman II* shatters another movie industry record: $24,009,272 in ticket sales in one week.

USA 18c
Disabled doesn't mean Unable

TUESDAY
June 30

Trampoline performer Richard Tison of France completes a world-record-breaking, triple-twisting triple-back somersault, which is broadcast on TV in West Germany.

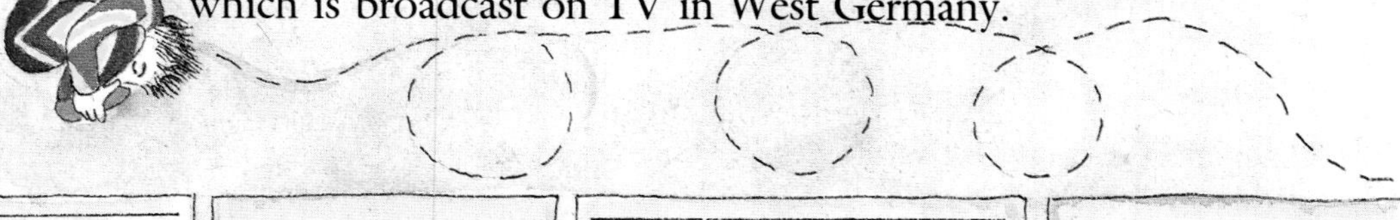

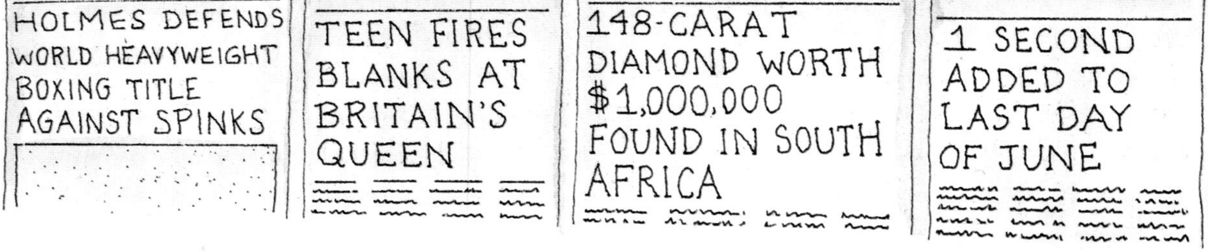
HOLMES DEFENDS WORLD HEAVYWEIGHT BOXING TITLE AGAINST SPINKS
TEEN FIRES BLANKS AT BRITAIN'S QUEEN
148-CARAT DIAMOND WORTH $1,000,000 FOUND IN SOUTH AFRICA
1 SECOND ADDED TO LAST DAY OF JUNE

July

*T*his month was named to honor Julius Caesar.

BIRTHSTONE *Ruby*

WEDNESDAY
July 1

16 convicts escape from a prison in Easton, Pennsylvania. • The first butterfly census in New York City is completed. The grand total: 401 butterflies (27 different species).

THURSDAY
July 2

50 goats are being moved by National Park Service helicopters from Olympic National Park to another part of Washington State. There were too many goats in the park, and they were eating all the flowers!

FRIDAY
July 3

Chris Evert Lloyd wins her 3d Wimbledon singles tennis title, defeating Hana Mandlikova. • 80 demonstrators protesting Ronald Reagan's policies are arrested at the White House.

SATURDAY
July 4

Independence Day • John McEnroe wins his 1st Wimbledon singles title, beating Bjorn Borg. • Jim Burkhart wins the International Cherry Pit Spitting Contest in Eau Claire, Michigan, with a mighty spit of 60 feet, 11¾ inches.

SUNDAY
July 5

100 British police officers are injured by rioters in Liverpool.

MONDAY
July 6

George Meegan, who is walking from the most southern point of the Americas to the most northern point, is in New York City today. He began his journey on January 26, 1977.

TUESDAY
July 7

The first solar-powered plane, the *Solar Challenger*, crosses the English Channel in 5½ hours. It weighs 210 pounds and its average speed is 30 miles per hour.

WHAT'S HOT IN 1981

- Rubik's Cube
- Lady Diana
- Headbands
- Designer chocolates
- Potato skins
- The Sony Walkman

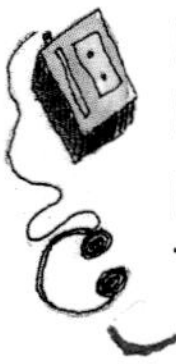

- Chipwich ice-cream sandwiches
- Camouflage jackets
- Feathered hats
- 3-D glasses
- Pac-man video game

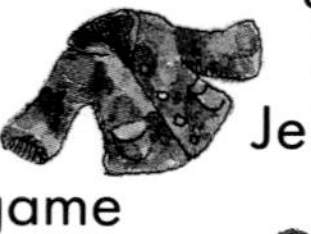

- Chu-Bops (chewable miniature records)
- Big League Chew (shredded bubble gum)
- Jelly beans

BIG
LEAGUE
CHEW

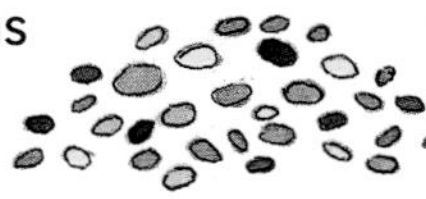

WHO ELSE WAS BORN IN JULY?

THURGOOD MARSHALL

U.S. judge, lawyer, associate justice of the U.S. Supreme Court
In 1967, Marshall became the first black to serve on the Supreme Court. He was also chief of the legal staff of the National Association for the Advancement of Colored People (NAACP).
BORN July 2, 1908, in Baltimore, Maryland

WEDNESDAY
July 8

TOP SWEET-CRET: England's Royal Navy is making a 200-pound cake for the wedding of Prince Charles and Lady Diana. No one is supposed to see it beforehand, so it is wrapped in plastic and kept on a shelf!

THURSDAY
July 9

Farming experts announce that hundreds of thousands of destructive Mediterranean fruit flies have accidentally been released in California, placing produce crops in danger.

FRIDAY
July 10

The governor of California orders that the state be sprayed by helicopter with a pesticide called malathion to help stop the spread of fruit flies.

SATURDAY
July 11

In Oslo, Norway, Steve Ovett of Great Britain wins the mile race with a time of 3 minutes, 49.25 seconds. Edwin Moses of the U.S. wins his 65th race in a row!

SUNDAY
July 12

A truck spills acid in Middletown, Pennsylvania, forcing 1,000 people to evacuate.

FUN FACT '81

Sooty terns produce a total of more than 1,000,000 eggs each year.

MONDAY
July 13

Protesters in Liverpool, England, throw tomatoes at Prime Minister Margaret Thatcher during her visit there.

TUESDAY
July 14

Marc Pajot of France arrives in England. He claims to have broken the world record for fastest west-to-east transatlantic sailing. His time: 9 days, 10 hours, 6 minutes.

WEDNESDAY
July 15

Jane Suzanne Mellor and Lori Love scale the 1,909-foot television tower in Wagoner, Oklahoma, which is 455 feet higher than the Sears Tower in Chicago. It takes them 5 hours; after reaching the top, they parachute down!

THURSDAY
July 16

In Denver, Colorado, Albert the alligator has been captured at last, after 28 days and nights of searching by zookeepers.

FRIDAY
July 17
Full Moon

Queen Elizabeth opens the world's longest suspension bridge—the Humber Estuary Bridge in Humberside, Great Britain. It is 1.37 miles long.

SATURDAY
July 18

The 12th annual gathering of the Jim Smith Society is held in Boiling Springs, Pennsylvania. Jim Smiths from 13 states and Canada attend.

SUNDAY
July 19

Bernard Hinault arrives in Paris and wins his 3d Tour de France bicycle race.

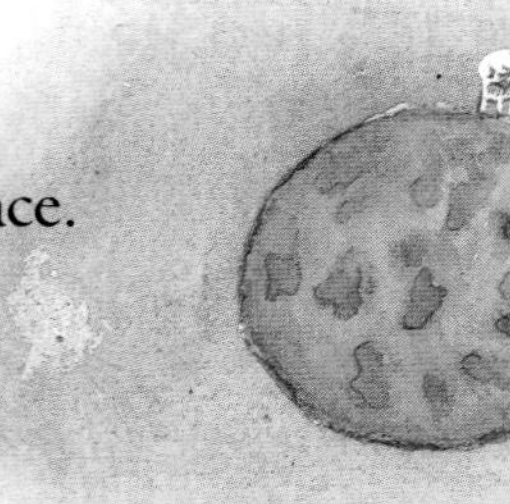

MONDAY
July 20

On this date in 1976, the U.S. space probe *Viking I* landed on Mars.

TUESDAY
July 21

7 major world leaders, including Prime Minister Zenko Suzuki of Japan, President François Mitterrand of France, and President Ronald Reagan, meet in Ottawa, Canada, to discuss world problems.

WEDNESDAY
July 22

CUBE CRAZE: More than 10,000,000 of the puzzle-game called Rubik's Cube have been sold worldwide!

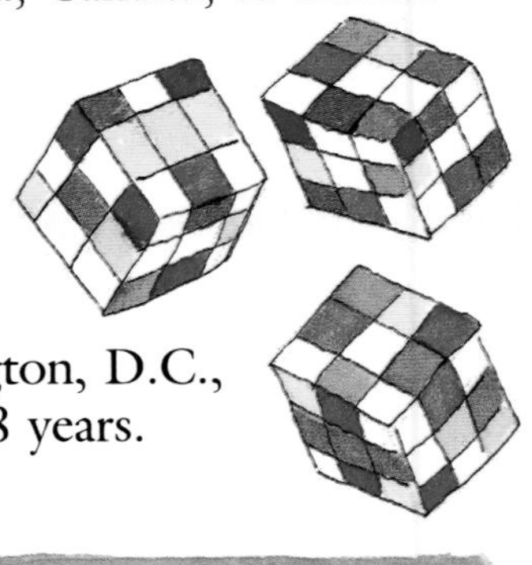

THURSDAY
July 23

WASHINGTON STAR
FINAL ISSUE

The *Washington Star*, a Washington, D.C., newspaper, shuts down after 128 years.

THANKS TO NIPPER

Approximately 750,000,000 people worldwide watch the wedding of Prince Charles and Lady Diana on TV on July 29. The live TV coverage is possible only becuase a tiny female ferret named Nipper has pulled a nylon thread through a small pipe that runs underground from Buckingham Palace. The thread is attached to a TV cable which is then pulled through the pipe so that the Royal procession can be televised.

COUNT ON RAIN

July 29 is Rain Day in Waynesburg, Pennsylvania. It has rained on this day for 93 out of the last 106 years. Every year, people wait to see whether or not it will rain on Rain Day—again. What's the weather like on July 29, 1981, in Waynesburg? What else: RAIN!

FRIDAY
July 24

The second mechanical heart ever to be placed in a human being is implanted in the body of a Dutch bus driver during an operation in Houston, Texas. The artificial heart is a little larger than a human heart.

SATURDAY
July 25

A huge catacomb is discovered in Italy by archaeologists. The underground passages cover an area the size of a football field and contain more than 1,000 grave niches.

SUNDAY
July 26

Mayor Edward Koch of New York City is saved from choking to death by a friend who performs the Heimlich maneuver on him.

MONDAY
July 27

A man in Brooklyn, New York, has been arrested for flying a kite at 1,000 feet. Police say it interferes with their helicopters.

TUESDAY
July 28

MAJOR SHAKER: An incredibly strong earthquake hits Iran—it's 7.3 on the Richter scale!

WEDNESDAY
July 29

The Prince of Wales marries Lady Diana Spencer at 11:00 A.M. in London, England. There are 2,500 guests at St. Paul's Cathedral; 750,000,000 people watch the ceremony on TV worldwide!

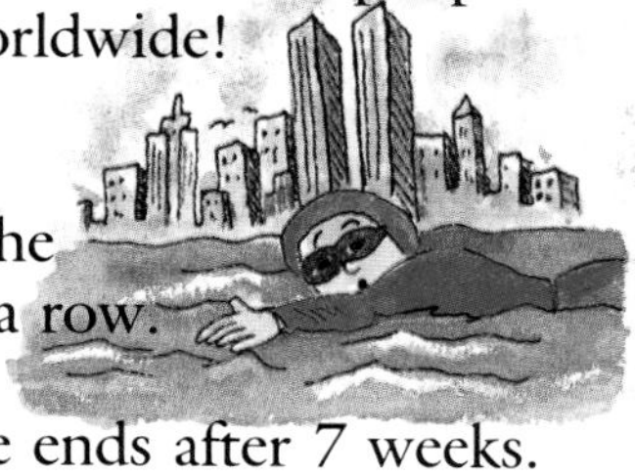

THURSDAY
July 30

Total eclipse of the sun, visible in much of the USSR • George Kauffman swims all the way around Manhattan for the 5th year in a row.

FRIDAY
July 31

PLAY BALL: The major league baseball strike ends after 7 weeks.

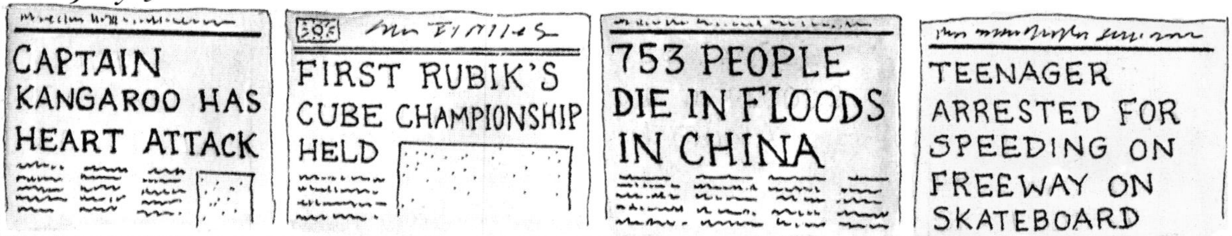
CAPTAIN KANGAROO HAS HEART ATTACK
FIRST RUBIK'S CUBE CHAMPIONSHIP HELD
753 PEOPLE DIE IN FLOODS IN CHINA
TEENAGER ARRESTED FOR SPEEDING ON FREEWAY ON SKATEBOARD

August

*A*ugust was named in honor of Roman emperor Augustus, whose lucky month it was.

BIRTHSTONE *Peridot*

SATURDAY
August 1

3 brothers arrive in Stamford, Connecticut, after bicycling for 43 days from their home in Seattle, Washington. • In Twinsburg, Ohio, 325 pairs of twins attend the 6th annual Twins Day.

SUNDAY
August 2

U.S. archaeologists digging in Israel report the discovery of the oldest known ark built for holding sacred scrolls. It dates back to the 3d century A.D.

MONDAY
August 3

Air controllers in the United States go on strike. 7,000 flights are grounded!

TUESDAY
August 4

3 Mediterranean fruit flies from California are found in East Tampa, Florida. Officials are worried that the Florida orange crop may be infested.

WEDNESDAY
August 5

President Reagan meets with President Anwar el-Sadat of Egypt to discuss problems in the Middle East.

THURSDAY
August 6

Tiger tamer John Cox and his assistant, Nina Pasko, are married. They ride on elephants to the wedding at the Ringling Brothers and Barnum & Bailey Circus World near Orlando, Florida.

FRIDAY
August 7

MOTH REPORT: Gypsy moth caterpillars have eaten 9,000,000 acres of tree leaves from Maine to Maryland.

SATURDAY
August 8

As of today, a team of international scientists has drilled 6,687 feet into the ice sheet in Greenland, in order to study the history of the earth's climate over the last 100,000 years.

SUNDAY
August 9

The baseball All-Star Game is won for the 10th time in a row by the National League, which defeats the American League 5–4. • In northern New Jersey, 1,400 people lose electricity when a squirrel climbs onto a power line!

WHO ELSE WAS BORN IN AUGUST?

MARIA MITCHELL

U.S. astronomer
She discovered a comet in 1847 and was the first woman to be elected to the American Academy of Arts and Sciences. She was professor of astronomy at Vassar College from 1865 to 1888.
BORN August 1, 1818, in Nantucket, Massachusetts

MONDAY
August 10
Postal workers in Canada go back to work. They have been on strike for 42 days.

TUESDAY
August 11
At New York City's Bronx Zoo, a cow gives birth to a gaur (a type of wild ox) as part of an experiment in embryo transplantation.

WEDNESDAY
August 12
John Erickson becomes the first person to swim the English Channel 3 times nonstop. Total time: 38 hours, 27 minutes!

THURSDAY
August 13
Italian police have broken up a counterfeiting ring in a raid in Rome. They found $1,000,000 in fake documents and bills.

FRIDAY
August 14
Steve Urner wins the cow-chip tossing at the Mountain Festival in Tehachapi, California. Winning distance: 266 feet.

SATURDAY
August 15
Full Moon

Voyager 2, now 7,200,000 miles away from Saturn, is sending back amazing photographs of the planet. • In France, 30 jewels worth $4,000,000 have been stolen from the villa of a Spanish princess.

SUNDAY
August 16
HORSE CENTS: A horse named Crown Velvet—the sister of a Triple Crown winner—is sold for $155,000 in East Rutherford, New Jersey.

MONDAY
August 17
Bill Neal paddles across the English Channel in a bathtub! It takes him 13 hours, 29 minutes.

VOYAGER VISITS SATURN

Saturn is 1 billion miles from Earth. On August 25, *Voyager 2* zooms close to Saturn. The space probe has traveled 1.24 billion miles in 4 years. One of the facts it discovers is that the temperature of Saturn is a freezing −300°F. Also, Saturn's atmosphere has winds that blow up to 1,000 miles per hour. No one can understand why the winds are so strong.

Saturn has 17 moons. Hyperion, the 8th-largest moon, looks like a battered potato!

TUESDAY
August 18

Researchers at the U.S. Department of Agriculture report that they have discovered a type of wild bee that produces polyester.

WEDNESDAY
August 19

In southern Arizona, there are so many caterpillars that they are making the roads slippery, and children are removing the insects by the bucketful.

THURSDAY
August 20

At the Bronx Zoo in New York City, a 180-pound elephant named Astor is born; his mother is an 11-year-old Indian elephant named Patty. Astor is the first elephant to be born in the New York area in 9,500 years!

FRIDAY
August 21

3 ministers on a golf course in Memphis, Tennessee, use their golf clubs to chase away a robber!

SATURDAY
August 22

Julian Nott crosses the English Channel in a hot-air balloon that runs on solar energy. It takes him less than 2 hours.

SUNDAY
August 23

Cameras on the space probe *Voyager 2* snap photos of Saturn's atmosphere. The pictures show 1,000-mile-per-hour winds and bluish storm clouds. The probe is only 1,400,000 miles from the planet.

MONDAY
August 24

A beluga whale is born at the New York Aquarium. She weighs 153 pounds and is the 4th beluga whale born in captivity.

TUESDAY
August 25

CLOSEST APPROACH: Speeding toward Saturn at 54,000 miles per hour, *Voyager 2* passes within 63,000 miles of the planet. The space probe sends back pictures of Saturn's rings and moons.

FUN FACT '81

An elephant can carry a 600-pound log with his trunk—or an object as small as a coin.

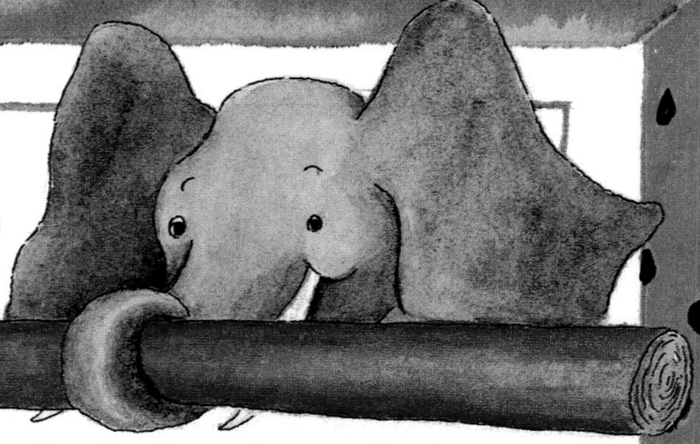

WEDNESDAY
August 26

Deep-sea divers find 1 of the 2 safes from the wreck of the *Andrea Doria* off Nantucket, Massachusetts. The ocean liner, which sank in 1956, is believed to have carried $1,000,000 in cash and jewels.

THURSDAY
August 27

Jose E. di Donato has invented a new game called Ping-Pong Poker. It uses paddles *and* cards!

FRIDAY
August 28

Sebastian Coe of Great Britain sets a new record for running the mile (3 minutes, 47.33 seconds) in Brussels, Belgium. This is the 3d time in 10 days that the world record has been broken.

SATURDAY
August 29

LAKE C.

Scientists and other experts gather in Shelburne, Vermont, to discuss the available evidence that there is really a "monster" in Lake Champlain.

SUNDAY
August 30

Taiwan wins the Little League baseball championship, defeating a team from Tampa, Florida. • More than 100 men and women from all over the world compete in the World Frisbee Disk Championship at the Rose Bowl in Pasadena, California.

MONDAY
August 31

1,300 reinforcements have been sent into southern Oregon to battle a fire that is raging out of control.

UGLY DOG
CONTEST
HELD IN
PETALUMA,
CALIFORNIA

120 ALLIGATORS
FLOWN TO SPA
IN ISRAEL

SCIENTISTS
WARN OF
GREENHOUSE
EFFECT

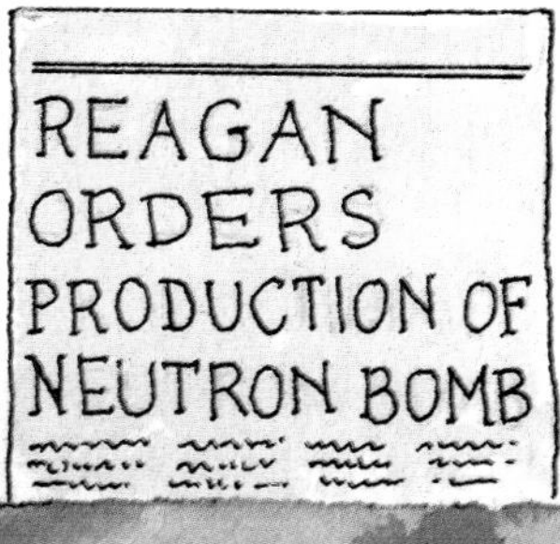
REAGAN
ORDERS
PRODUCTION OF
NEUTRON BOMB

September

*T*he name September comes from the Latin *septem*, meaning "seven." This was the seventh month of the old Roman calendar.

BIRTHSTONE *Sapphire*

TUESDAY
September 1

Happy birthday to the famous boxer Rocky Marciano, who was born on this day in 1923, and to comedian Lily Tomlin, born on September 1, 1936.

WEDNESDAY
September 2

Police in London recover a valuable painting by Rembrandt that was stolen from the Dulwich Picture Gallery in Great Britain on August 14.

THURSDAY
September 3

NEWS "FLASH": David Bergstein has invented a device that makes sparks during roller-skating. When the skater tilts backward, the sparks fly!

FRIDAY
September 4

• Mbabane
SWAZILAND

The 82-year-old king of Swaziland, Sobhuza II, who is called the Lion of Swaziland, celebrates the 60th year of his reign with a big ceremony and party. The guests include 29 of his wives and many of his 150 children.

SATURDAY
September 5

A rare jabiru stork is spotted in Corpus Christi, Texas, by a bird-watcher from Austin.

SUNDAY
September 6

First Lady Nancy Reagan and her staff put up and decorate a Christmas tree in the family quarters of the White House. Photographers are coming to take pictures for a magazine article about Christmas in the White House.

MONDAY
September 7

Labor Day • Hurricane Floyd races toward Bermuda with wind gusts of up to 110 knots.

TUESDAY
September 8

SUMMER VACATION CONTINUES: There's no school yet for kids in Philadelphia, Pennsylvania. The teachers are on strike.

FAIR PAY FOR EDUCATION
ON STRIKE
FAIR PAY FOR TEACHERS
MORE PAY!
ON STRIKE

WHO ELSE WAS BORN IN SEPTEMBER?

SAMUEL ADAMS

American Revolutionary leader and statesman He was one of the signers of the Declaration of Independence and organized the famous Boston Tea Party. He also served as governor of Massachusetts (1794–97) and as a member of the Continental Congress from 1776 to 1781.
BORN September 27, 1722, in Boston, Massachusetts

WEDNESDAY
September 9
In Tasmania, 160 pilot whales beach themselves, while hundreds of volunteers try to save them before they die. • Alligator season opens in Louisiana. For the first time in 18 years, it's legal to hunt alligators.

THURSDAY
September 10
John Carta parachutes out of an airplane and lands on top of the World Trade Center in New York City.

FRIDAY
September 11

The Bean Soup Festival is held in McClure, Pennsylvania. • In Montgomery, Indiana, the Daviess County Turkey Trot Festival takes place, featuring turkey races and a contest for best-dressed turkey.

SATURDAY
September 12
Bird-watchers from all over the U.S. come to Corpus Christi, Texas, to see the rare jabiru stork, the first one seen in the U.S. since 1971. The stork can grow to a height of 57 inches.

SUNDAY
September 13
Grandparents' Day • U.S. Open singles tennis championships are won by John McEnroe and Tracy Austin.

MONDAY
September 14
Full Moon
BABY BEAR BIRTH: In Peking, China, a baby panda is born at the Peking Zoo.

TUESDAY
September 15
In Alberta, Canada, the world's largest shopping center opens. It covers an area of 5,200,000 square feet and holds 840 stores and services.

WEDNESDAY
September 16

11 protestors are arrested at the Diablo Canyon nuclear power plant in California. They are demonstrating against operating a nuclear power plant so close to an undersea fault. So far, 558 people have been arrested at this plant.

THURSDAY
September 17

Paleontologist Farish A. Jenkins, Jr., announces the discovery in Arizona of a fossil jaw from a tiny shrewlike animal. It is 180,000,000 years old.

FRIDAY
September 18

Forrest Sondrud catches a specially tagged salmon near Seattle, Washington. The fish, which was worth $1,000,000 if caught during a September 6 fishing contest, is now worth only $10,000.

SATURDAY
September 19

FISH OUT OF WATER? An 8½-foot-long, 300-pound blue shark is found on a sidewalk in the East Village in New York City.

SUNDAY
September 20

Divers have raised more than 100 gold bars from the wreck of the British cruiser *Edinburgh*, which sank on May 2, 1942, off northern Norway. The gold is worth about $20,000,000.

MONDAY
September 21

The Senate confirms the appointment of Sandra Day O'Connor to the U.S. Supreme Court. She is the first woman member of the Supreme Court.

TUESDAY
September 22

Autumn equinox • The TGV, a new high-speed train which can go up to 320 miles per hour, begins service in France today. President Mitterrand goes for the first ride, from Paris to Lyons. The 300-mile trip takes the TGV only 2 hours, 32 minutes.

WEDNESDAY
September 23

In Washington, D.C., at the largest computer conference ever held, IBM introduces a new personal computer to 11,000 experts. IBM has also produced a new memory chip that can store 288,000 bits of information.

JELLY BEANS IN THE WHITE HOUSE

The new president of the United States, Ronald Reagan, loves jelly beans. It is rumored that he has some every day. Jelly beans are an oval-shaped candy with a hard sugar coating. President Reagan's favorite kind are Jelly Bellies, which have liquid in the center!

FUN FACT '81

The oldest living tree is a bristlecone pine in California; it has been growing there for 4,600 years.

THURSDAY
September 24

Divers exploring the wreck of the HMS *Edinburgh* have recovered an astounding 225 gold bars, worth about $45,000,000!

FRIDAY
September 25

American Indian Day • 2 Soviet reconnaissance planes are intercepted by the U.S. Air Force off the North Carolina coast. The Soviet planes are escorted out of U.S. air space.

SATURDAY
September 26

11-year-old Dougie Hsieh of New York City becomes the youngest Life Master of contract bridge in the world.

SUNDAY
September 27

New archaeological proof has been found which shows that there was a population explosion in Venezuela from 800 B.C. to A.D. 400.

MONDAY
September 28

Rosh Hashanah begins at sunset. • Mount Pavlof, a volcano in Alaska, erupts with a large flow of lava. Ash and rocks spurt from the crater.

TUESDAY
September 29

Oweee!

A Canadian physician reports that playing with the puzzle-game Rubik's Cube can cause a condition called Cuber's thumb—in other words, a sore thumb!

WEDNESDAY
September 30

The liftoff of space shuttle *Columbia* is delayed due to a fuel spill. The fuel has dissolved some of the glue that holds the shuttle's surface tiles in place.

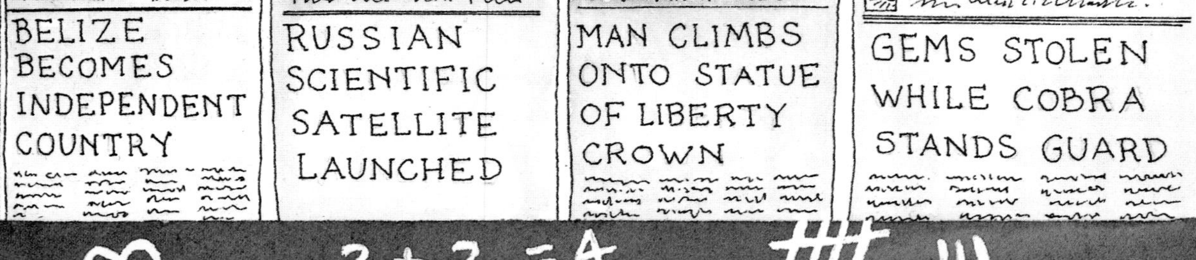
BELIZE BECOMES INDEPENDENT COUNTRY
RUSSIAN SCIENTIFIC SATELLITE LAUNCHED
MAN CLIMBS ONTO STATUE OF LIBERTY CROWN
GEMS STOLEN WHILE COBRA STANDS GUARD

October

*O*ctober was the eighth month of the old Roman calendar; the name is from the Latin *octo*, meaning "eight."

BIRTHSTONE *Opal*

THURSDAY
October 1
One of the several pairs of ruby red shoes worn by Dorothy in the movie *The Wizard of Oz* are sold for $12,000 in New York City. • Avalanche warnings in the Swiss Alps!

FRIDAY
October 2
Astronomers have discovered what looks like a huge hole in space, 300,000,000 light-years wide. Experts are baffled.

SATURDAY
October 3
Hundreds flock to the World's Chicken Pluckin' Championship in Spring Hill, Florida. It features Rooster Crowing, Baby Chick, Old Hen, and Miss Drumstick contests, as well as the chicken-plucking event.

SUNDAY
October 4

OFFICIAL
PHOTO OF CHAMP

MORE MONSTER NEWS: Officials at Port Henry, New York, report that 3 dozen people this year have seen the Lake Champlain monster.

MONDAY
October 5
SPECIAL DELIVERY: Several suitcases fall from an airplane onto the roofs of 2 buildings in Newark, New Jersey. The plane was on its way to Washington, D.C., but someone left a cargo door open.

TUESDAY
October 6
NASA launches a satellite called the *Solar Mesosphere Explorer* to study the ozone layer. It will pass over the North and South poles once every 95 minutes.

WEDNESDAY
October 7
Off the coast of Norway, the underwater salvage operation of the wreck of the cruiser *Edinburgh* finally comes to an end; 460 gold ingots have been recovered.

CASH TRASH

A rotting burlap bag filled with thousands of dollars is found in Windsor, Connecticut, on October 24. Some paper receipts show that the money is from a payroll robbery that took place in 1957! $66,573 was stolen.

WHO ELSE WAS BORN IN OCTOBER?

MARTINA NAVRATILOVA

U.S. tennis player
She defected to the U.S. in 1974 and became one of the U.S.'s best players. She won the Wimbledon Women's singles title in 1978 and 1979, and would go on to set a record by winning it 6 straight years (1982–1987).
BORN October 10, 1956, in Prague, Czechoslovakia

THURSDAY
October 8
Yom Kippur • At a hotel in Paris, France, 2 thieves steal jewels valued at $3,000,000 from a couple staying there, including a 45-carat diamond ring worth at least $2,000,000.

FRIDAY
October 9
In Costa Mesa, California, Fred Gorell and John Shoecraft take off in a helium-filled balloon called the *Super Chicken III* to fly nonstop across the U.S.

SATURDAY
October 10
TURKEY TOSS: At the annual Turkey Trot Festival in Yellville, Arkansas, a small plane flies low over the cheering crowd and tosses out flapping turkeys.

SUNDAY
October 11
Astronomers have discovered the hottest spot in the Solar System: a cloud of gas circling Saturn that is 300 times hotter than the outer regions of the Sun.

MONDAY
October 12
Columbus Day • The helium-filled *Super Chicken III* lands on Blackbeard Island, Georgia, becoming the first balloon to cross the U.S. It traveled 2,515 miles.

TUESDAY
October 13
Full Moon

Pianist and comedian Victor Borge has been knighted by the consul general of Finland. This is his 4th honor of this kind; he's already been knighted in Denmark, Sweden, and Norway!

WEDNESDAY
October 14
3 members of a North American research team attempt to climb Mount Everest but fail because of bad weather.

THURSDAY
October 15
In Herefordshire, England, 60 sheep have been fitted with false teeth!

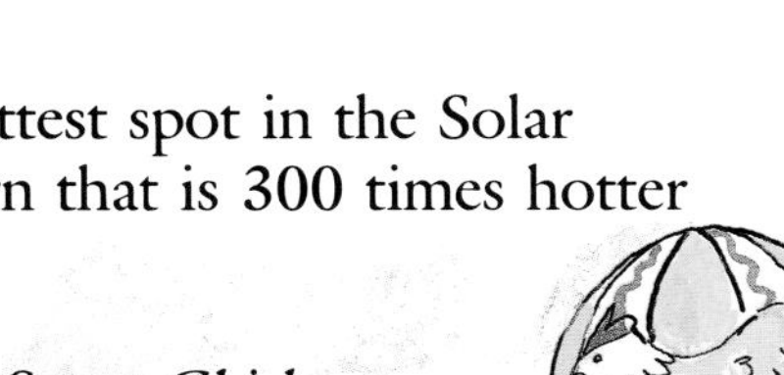

TOP TEN NAMES FOR BOYS AND GIRLS IN 1981*

BOYS		GIRLS	
1 Michael	6 Anthony	1 Jennifer	6 Elizabeth
2 Christopher	7 John	2 Jessica	7 Lisa
3 David	8 Daniel	3 Melissa	8 Tiffany
4 Jason	9 Robert	4 Nicole	9 Christina
5 Joseph	10 James	5 Michelle	10 Danielle

*Source: *New York Times* list of most popular names in New York City.

FRIDAY
October 16
Happy birthday to Noah Webster, born in 1758. He is known as the father of the American dictionary.

WEBSTER'S
DICTIONARY

SATURDAY
October 17
In Washington, D.C., President and Mrs. Reagan attend the celebration of the 40th anniversary of the USO (United Service Organization). It was founded in 1941 to provide entertainment for people in the military.

SUNDAY
October 18
You Can Do the Cube, a 112-page book by 13-year-old Patrick Bossert, is at the top of the *New York Times* best-seller list. It has sold 750,000 copies so far.

MONDAY
October 19
Astronomers at the National Science Foundation announce that they have found a star 20 times hotter than the sun. It's a white dwarf in the constellation Ursa Major.

TUESDAY
October 20
Buie and Sasha, 2 dolphins that live in the New York Aquarium, have flown south for the winter. They went by jet!

WEDNESDAY
October 21

One of the 3 who had to turn back on October 14, Christopher Kopcjynski of Spokane, Washington, finally reaches the top of Mount Everest, where he conducts medical tests on his heart and lungs.

THURSDAY
October 22
Frederick P. Deluca of Ames, Iowa, has invented an electronic earring that lights up in the dark—it sparkles better than a real gem!

FRIDAY
October 23
Leaders from 22 countries meet in Cancún, Mexico, to discuss worldwide economic aid. • The swallows depart from San Juan Capistrano in California.

SATURDAY
October 24
United Nations Day • In London, 150,000 people march to protest nuclear weapons.

FUN FACT '81

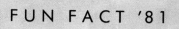

There are 1,370 chimpanzees in the U.S.

SUNDAY
October 25

16,000 people run in the New York Marathon in New York City; Alberto Salazar wins with a world-record time of 2 hours, 8 minutes, 13 seconds, and Allison Roe beats the women's world record with her time of 2 hours, 25 minutes, 28 seconds.

MONDAY
October 26

100 years ago today, the famous gunfight at the O.K. Corral took place in Tombstone, Arizona.

TUESDAY
October 27

A Soviet submarine armed with nuclear weapons runs aground close to a Swedish naval base.

WEDNESDAY
October 28

SPY EXCHANGE: West Germany and East Germany make a trade, exchanging their convicted spies. • In New York City, the Los Angeles Dodgers win baseball's World Series, beating the New York Yankees 9–2, in the 6th game.

THURSDAY
October 29

Yukigiro Yanagisawa and Hiroshi Aota reach the top of the south face of Annapurna I in the Himalaya Mountains. They are the first people to climb this 26,700-foot peak.

FRIDAY
October 30

The Soviet Union launches an unmanned spacecraft called *Venera 13*, which is expected to reach Venus by next March. • Great Britain passes a law that creates 3 different categories of citizenship.

SATURDAY
October 31

Halloween • 13-year-old Anthony M. Sarkis, Jr., in North Adams, Massachusetts, watches as a red fireball streaks across the sky and a glowing red meteorite the size of a baseball lands in his backyard. It leaves a crater a foot wide!

ANWAR EL-SADAT, PRESIDENT OF EGYPT, KILLED
LANDSLIDES IN CHINA LEAVE 100,000 HOMELESS
AGENTS SEIZE $2,500,000 IN COUNTERFEIT MONEY

November

*N*ovember was the ninth month of the old Roman calendar. The name comes from the Latin *novem*, meaning "nine."

BIRTHSTONE *Topaz*

SUNDAY
November 1

Daniel Goodwin, the man who climbed the Sears Tower on Memorial Day, tries to scale the John Hancock Building in Chicago, Illinois. His suction cups don't work well on this building; fire fighters have to rescue Spider-Man.

MONDAY
November 2

In Saudi Arabia, schools are closed today so that pupils and teachers can pray for rain.

TUESDAY
November 3

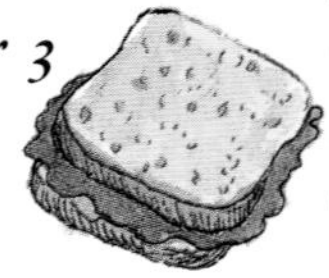

Mayor Edward Koch is reelected mayor of New York City in a landslide vote. • Sandwich Day, in honor of the inventor of the sandwich, John Montague, the 4th earl of Sandwich, who was born on November 3, 1718.

WEDNESDAY
November 4

The launch of space shuttle *Columbia* is postponed just 31 seconds before takeoff.

THURSDAY
November 5

In baseball, pitcher Rollie Fingers of the Milwaukee Brewers has been named the American League winner of the Cy Young Award.

FRIDAY
November 6

The U.S. Department of the Interior announces that a black-footed ferret, an animal thought to be extinct, has been captured in a prairie dog colony in Wyoming. A tracking collar is put around its neck and it is set free.

FLOWERS IN SPACE

When U.S. space shuttle *Columbia* lifts off for its 2d trip into space on November 12, it has 85 extra passengers on board—85 dwarf sunflower seeds, each planted in its own separate cylinder. The purpose of the experiment is to find out what kind of moisture is needed to grow seedlings where there is no gravity. Scientists are also hoping to discover how gravity affects the way a plant grows.

TOP TEN SINGLES OF 1981*

1	"The Tide Is High"	Blondie
2	"Celebration"	Kool and the Gang
3	"9 to 5"	Dolly Parton
4	"I Love a Rainy Night"	Eddie Rabbit
5	"Keep on Loving You"	REO Speedwagon
6	"Rapture"	Blondie
7	"Kiss on My List"	Daryl Hall and John Oates
8	"Morning Train"	Sheena Easton
9	"Bette Davis Eyes"	Kim Carnes
10	"Stars On"	Stars on 45

*Source: *Billboard.*

SATURDAY
November 7

Lizards, frogs, and a terrapin are stolen from the reptile house at the London Zoo in Great Britain.

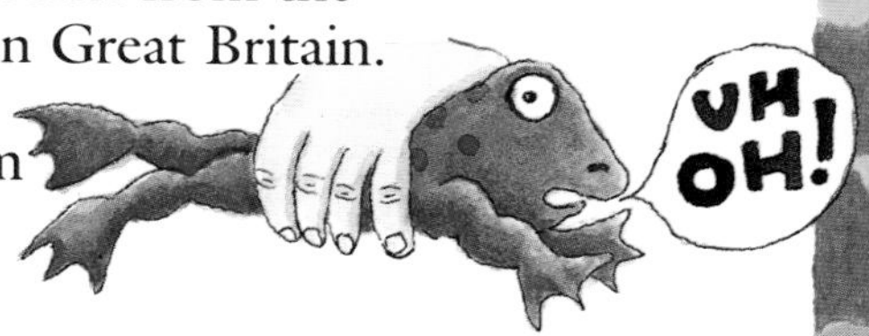
UH OH!

SUNDAY
November 8

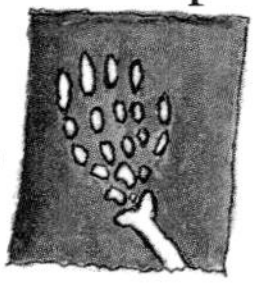

On this day in 1895, Wilhelm Roentgen discovered X rays.

MONDAY
November 9

A 26-story-high, helium-filled balloon called the *Double Eagle V* lifts off from Nagashima, Japan. Its 4 passengers—Ben Abruzzo, Larry Newman, Ron Clark, and Rocky Aoki—hope to be the first to cross the Pacific Ocean in a balloon.

TUESDAY
November 10

At 8:00 A.M., the countdown begins again for the launching of the 2d flight of *Columbia* from Cape Canaveral, Florida. • Ornithologist Jared Diamond reports that he has discovered a yellow-fronted gardener bowerbird in New Guinea.

WEDNESDAY
November 11

Full Moon

Veteran's Day • Baseball's Fernando Valenzuela of the Los Angeles Dodgers wins the National League Cy Young Award.

THURSDAY
November 12

Today *Columbia* becomes the first spacecraft in the world to be launched twice. • The *Double Eagle V* crash-lands in Covello, California. It has traveled 5,208.68 miles, setting a new distance record for a balloon.

FUN FACT '81

Every year, a moose grows 7-foot antlers in 10 weeks, then sheds them.

FRIDAY
November 13

The *Columbia* astronauts are ordered to cut short their 5-day mission, due to a faulty fuel cell.

SATURDAY
November 14

Columbia lands at Edwards Air Force Base in California after a 2-day space flight. • President Reagan goes on a wild turkey hunt in San Antonio, Texas.

SUNDAY
November 15

A scientist in Utah, James Jansen, has found part of a skeleton of the world's oldest bird, the *Paleopteryx thomsoni*. It's 140,000,000 years old!

VOLLEYBALL NEWS

Volleyball is a game usually played by two teams of six people. To play the game, a large ball is volleyed—batted or hit back and forth across a high net—using any part of the body above the waist. Players can even use their heads! The side that fails to return the ball across the net, or that hits the ball out of the court, loses a point.

Volleyball was invented in 1895 by W. G. Morgan at the YMCA in Holyoke, Massachusetts. It has been an Olympic event since 1964. In November, 1981, in Osaka, Japan, China wins the women's World Cup in volleyball for the very first time, beating both the U. S. and Japan.

MONDAY
November 16

Scientists at the Massachusetts Institute of Technology have created a new type of polio virus that could lead to the development of a new vaccine. • Children's Book Week begins.

TUESDAY
November 17

Mike Schmidt of baseball's Philadelphia Phillies is voted Most Valuable Player of the Year in the National League.

WEDNESDAY
November 18

The Tecopa pupfish is officially extinct, as of today. It used to live in the rivers of Death Valley in California. • A 50-pound turkey is presented to President Reagan at the White House.

To: President Reagan

WHO ELSE WAS BORN IN NOVEMBER?

INDIRA GANDHI

Indian political leader
The prime minister and Congress party leader of India from 1966 to 1977, she was reelected in 1980. She was the first woman prime minister of India.
BORN November 19, 1917, in Alahabad, India

THURSDAY *November 19* — In Chicago, Illinois, Hollywood stuntman Daniel Goodwin is ordered not to climb any more buildings—with or without his Spider-Man suit.

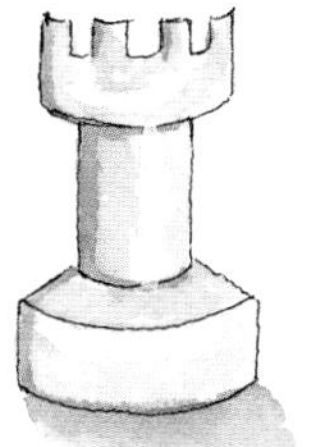

FRIDAY *November 20* — In Italy, Anatoly Karpov wins the world chess championship, defeating Viktor Korchnoi of Switzerland in the 18th game. • Blizzards pound the Midwest.

SATURDAY *November 21* — Minami-dake volcano in southern Japan erupts, sending ash 8,000 feet into the air! It's the 192d time it's erupted this year.

SUNDAY *November 22* — For sale in Dallas, Texas: a robot that can dust, clean, serve refreshments, and walk the dog.

MONDAY *November 23* — Australia–United States Boomerang Match in Sydney, Australia. • Anniversary of the birth of Billy the Kid, in 1859, and Boris Karloff, in 1887.

TUESDAY *November 24* — The director of the Washington Park Zoo in Portland, Oregon, orders 4 harbor seals to be set free. The seals have been eating the coins, flashcubes, and other objects that visitors throw them and have developed a sickness called hardware disease.

WEDNESDAY *November 25* — In New York City, a black-belt karate expert—who happens to be in line at the bank—captures a bank robber as he tries to leave with stolen money. • Rollie Fingers of baseball's Milwaukee Brewers is named Most Valuable Player of the American League.

SCORE ONE FOR THE BIRDS

On November 10, 1981, a bird expert reports finding a very rare bird—a yellow-fronted gardener bowerbird—that the world had thought was extinct. Bird lovers are very happy this bird was found since the number of threatened and endangered species is always increasing.

Human beings are believed to be the major cause of birds becoming extinct. About 100 species of birds have disappeared from the planet since the year 1600, including the dodo bird, the passenger pigeon, and the Carolina parakeet.

THURSDAY
November 26

Thanksgiving Day • A priceless solid gold pre-Columbian ceremonial knife is stolen from a museum in Lima, Peru.

FRIDAY
November 27

Scientists have found the world's oldest religious shrine in El Juyo Cave in northern Spain. It's 14,000 years old and has a sculpture of a head that is a cat on one side and a human on the other.

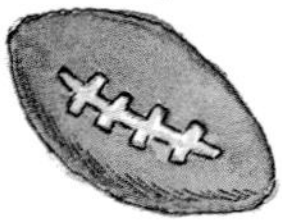

SATURDAY
November 28

Coach Paul Bryant of the University of Alabama wins his 315th game, setting a new record for college football coaching wins.

SUNDAY
November 29

At the Bronx Zoo in New York City, a special gourmet feast has been prepared for the animals to enjoy, featuring a "dinosaur" made out of pineapples, a "snake" made out of apples, and a "turkey" made out of grain.

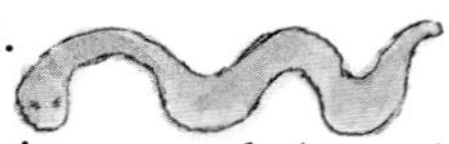

MONDAY
November 30

Dave Righetti of the New York Yankees is named American League Rookie of the Year. • In the largest computer chip theft in history, 500,000 chips worth $2,700,000 are found missing from a company in Silicon Valley, California.

MILWAUKEE ZOO'S
GORILLA
SAMSON
DIES

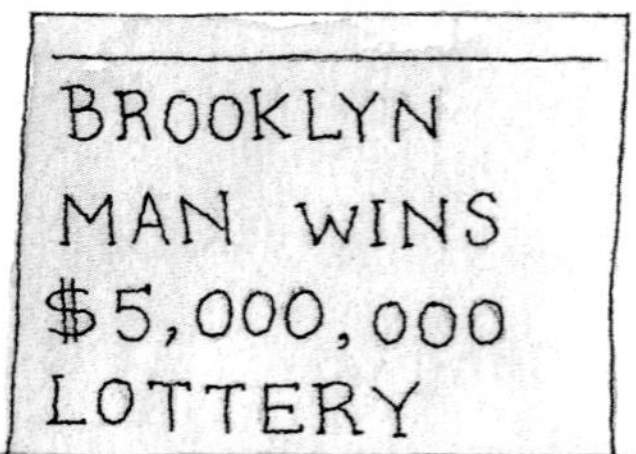
BROOKLYN
MAN WINS
$5,000,000
LOTTERY

PRISON
WARDEN
ARRESTED FOR
SHOPLIFTING

December

*D*ecember used to be the tenth month of the year (the Latin *decem* means "ten"). The old Roman calendar began with March.

BIRTHSTONE *Turquoise*

TUESDAY
December 1
A blizzard pounds the Midwest with 50-mile-an-hour winds and blinding snow. Many roads and schools are closed in parts of Nebraska, South Dakota, Minnesota, and Iowa.

WEDNESDAY
December 2
Fernando Valenzuela, left-handed pitcher for the Los Angeles Dodgers, is voted National League Rookie of the Year.

THURSDAY
December 3
3 fish that may be of a never-before-seen species are accidentally caught near the floor of the Pacific Ocean by a deep-sea-diving submarine. The fish are 10 inches long and white.

FRIDAY
December 4
President Reagan gives permission for the CIA to spy inside the U.S. Until now, the CIA was supposed to spy only in foreign countries.

SATURDAY
December 5

The Heisman Trophy for outstanding college football player is awarded to University of Southern California tailback Marcus Allen.

SUNDAY
December 6
The White House is closed this weekend while Mrs. Reagan and staff decorate it for Christmas. • Dorothy Miles catches a record-breaking 6-pound, 2-ounce bigeye trevally in Papua New Guinea.

TOY BOX '81

- Smurf
- Barbie
- Tiny Tears
- Patti Playpal
- *Star Wars* toys
- Strawberry Shortcake
- Clyde's Car Crusher
- Pork Chop Hill play set
- Little People

TOP TOY OF '81—RUBIK'S CUBE

Rubik's Cube is a multicolored, three-dimensional plastic puzzle with smaller cubes that rotate to form a larger cube. It was invented by Erno Rubik, who is a teacher of architecture and design in Hungary. The object of the game is to turn all the smaller cubes so that they are back to their original place, with a solid color showing on each side. Rubik's Cube, like all cubes, has 6 sides. There are 43 quintillion possible positions!

Rubik's Cube is so popular that some companies come out with their own versions: the Magic Puzzler, Perfect Puzzler, Wonderful Puzzler, Challenge Puzzler, and Le Cube.

MONDAY
December 7

Dr. Roy P. Mackal, who went to Africa to search for the legendary half-elephant, half-dragon beast called the mokele-mbembe, returns to Chicago, Illinois. He found a new species of snake and some strange footprints in the jungle, but no mokele-mbembe!

TUESDAY
December 8

Hijackers seize 3 jetliners in flight and force them to fly to Cuba. The passengers are released.

WEDNESDAY
December 9

2 boats pushing barges that are carrying fuel collide in the Ohio River, causing a huge explosion and fire that burns for more than 20 hours.

THURSDAY
December 10

Human Rights Day • The U.S. government reports that 12,300,000 people, a record high number, are enrolled in college this fall. That's 126,000 more than last year.

FRIDAY
December 11
Full Moon

U.S. SMURF TURF: 30,000,000 Smurfs have been sold since the toy arrived from Europe in 1979.

SATURDAY
December 12

In Miami, Florida, the Metrozoo officially opens, with 160 acres of land and 53 exhibits!

SUNDAY
December 13

In Cincinnati, Ohio, the Davis Cup international tennis competition is won by the U.S., which defeats Argentina. • A state of martial law is declared in Poland.

WHO ELSE WAS BORN IN DECEMBER?

CLARA BARTON

U.S. humanitarian
She founded the American Red Cross in 1881 and became its first president. She was called the Angel of the Battlefield during the Civil War for organizing a service that brought care and supplies to the wounded soldiers.
BORN December 25, 1821, in Oxford, Massachusetts

MONDAY
December 14
In Italy, in the men's slalom, Steve and Phil Mahre, twins from Yakima, Washington, become the first brothers and the first Americans to finish first and second in a World Cup ski race. Steve's time: 1 minute, 44.64 seconds; Phil's time: 1 minute, 44.72 seconds.

TUESDAY
December 15
Bill of Rights Day • The Iraqi embassy in Beirut, Lebanon, is bombed. An anonymous caller says the bombing is on behalf of Kurdish rebels in Iraq.

BOMB

WEDNESDAY
December 16
In Lagos de Moreno, Mexico, 5 men with guns hold up 2 banks, one right after the other! They escape with $3,600,000 in cash.

THURSDAY
December 17
Wright Brothers Day • General James L. Dozier of the U.S. is kidnapped in Italy by the Red Brigades, a terrorist organization.

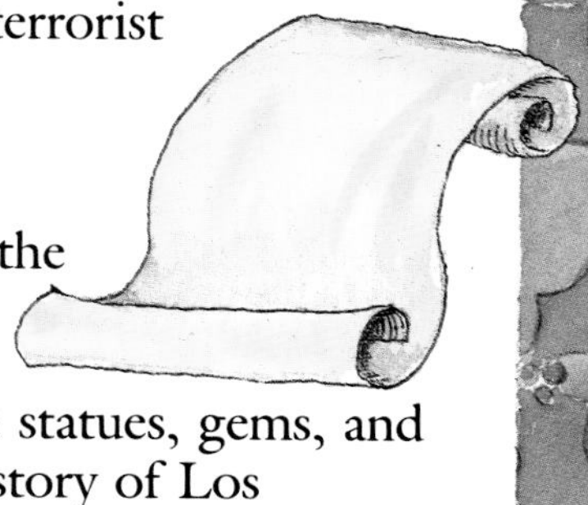

FRIDAY
December 18
On this day in 1865, slavery was abolished in the U.S., when the 34th state approved the 13th amendment to the Constitution.

SATURDAY
December 19
Thieves in Los Angeles steal $4,500,000 in statues, gems, and cash, one of the largest burglaries in the history of Los Angeles. One of the stolen jewels is a $400,000 sapphire.

FUN FACT '81

There are 4,500,000 twins in the U.S.

SUNDAY
December 20

The Polish ambassador to the U.S. is granted political asylum in the United States.

MONDAY
December 21

Hanukkah • Also the winter solstice. Winter begins at 5:51 P.M. EST. • Today is Forefathers Day; in 1620, 103 Pilgrims on the *Mayflower* landed at what is now Plymouth, Massachusetts.

TUESDAY
December 22

A horse named John Henry is named horse of the year. He's the world's richest racehorse, with winnings of $3,022,810.

WEDNESDAY
December 23

CHRISTMAS INSPIRATION: Stanley W. Urban of Sparta, New Jersey, has patented a green crystal gemstone that glows red under artificial light.

THURSDAY
December 24

Christmas Eve • On December 24, 1818, the music for "Silent Night" was composed by Frank Gruber; it was to accompany the original words by Josef Mohr.

WATCH OUT FOR THAT SINKHOLE

A sinkhole is a funnel-shaped dent or hole in the ground which tends to start small and get bigger. Sinkholes are caused by a collapsing underground cavern or by a large crack in the subterranean rock. While they are growing, they tend to swallow up objects which may be nearby. Sinkholes, which are also called sinks, swallow holes, dolines, or poljes, can be as large as several miles in diameter. They are often found in areas where there is a lot of limestone in the earth.

In 1981, a sinkhole in Florida is so big, it swallows a whole house, some cars—and a swimming pool!

FRIDAY
December 25

Christmas • The rattlesnake census of the state of New Jersey is in—there are 7 active rattlesnake dens.

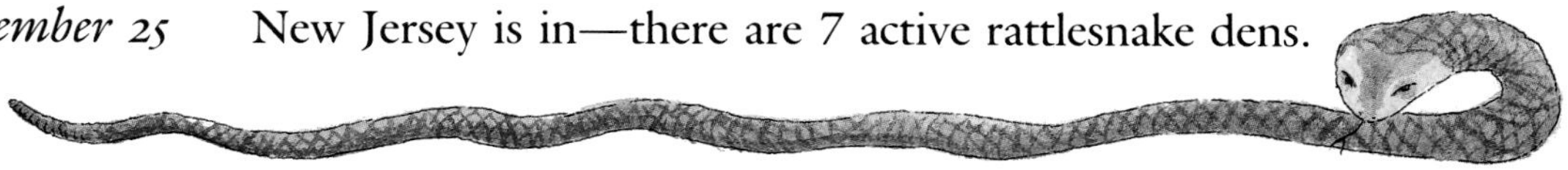

SATURDAY
December 26

In Indianapolis, Indiana, Ginger Steward opens a bag of potato chips and finds a wallet! It belongs to Theodore Kelley, who dropped it (by accident) onto a conveyor belt in a potato chip factory in Terre Haute, Indiana.

SUNDAY
December 27

The Doo Dah Parade is held in Pasadena, California. It features a team of crutch-walking nurses, a power-lawnmower drill team, a synchronized-briefcase drill team, and a book-clapping band!

MONDAY
December 28

The first U.S. test-tube baby, Elizabeth Carr, is born at Norfolk General Hospital in Virginia.

TUESDAY
December 29

DOG TAGS? The U.S. military is looking for dogs from across the nation to join the military. Canines are welcome in all branches of the service: Air Force, Navy, Marines, Army—even the FBI!

WEDNESDAY
December 30

The U.S. Department of Agriculture reports that Newcastle's disease, deadly to chickens and turkeys, has been found in parrots in Colorado Springs, Colorado.

THURSDAY
December 31

New Year's Eve • The famous globe in New York City's Times Square descends to bring in the new year—but this time it's a 6-foot-tall lighted apple! It cost $90,000 to transform it into the Big Apple.

1982!

2 EARTHQUAKES RATTLE FAIRBANKS, ALASKA
ARGENTINA'S PRESIDENT OUSTED
SIGHTSEERS IN INDIA STAMPEDE
TROUBLE IN EL SALVADOR

1
2
3
4

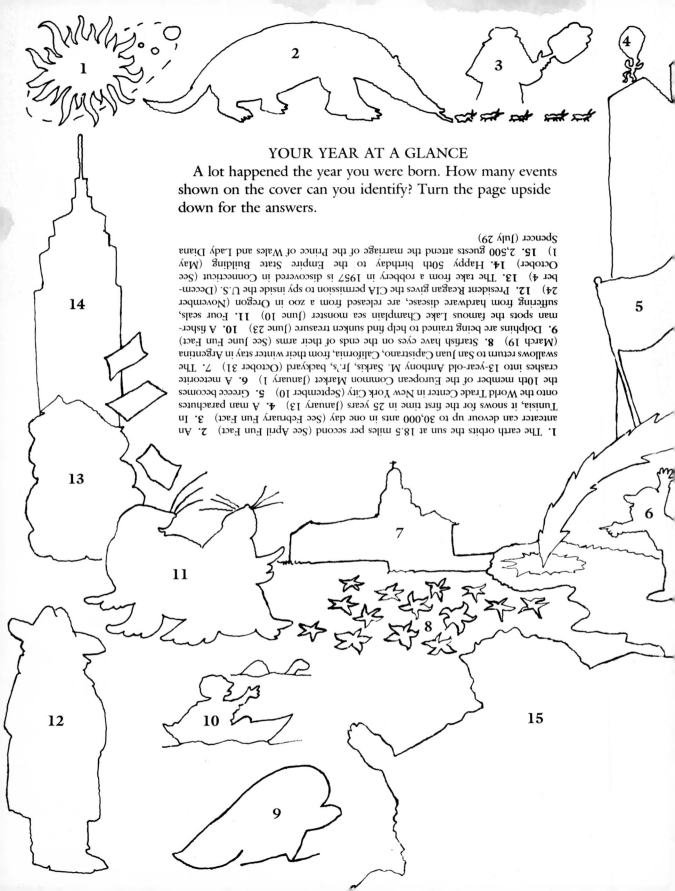

YOUR YEAR AT A GLANCE

A lot happened the year you were born. How many events shown on the cover can you identify? Turn the page upside down for the answers.

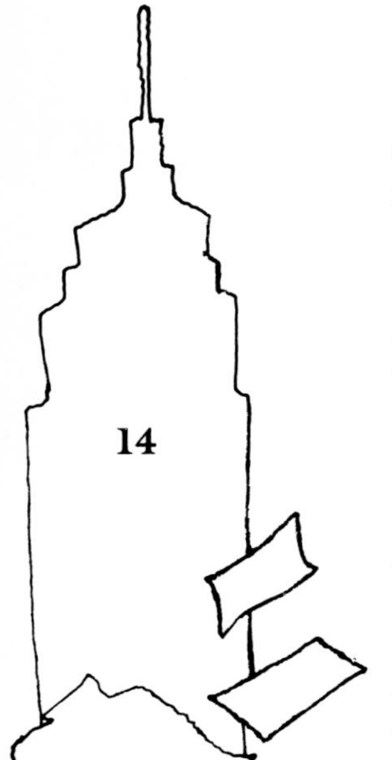
14

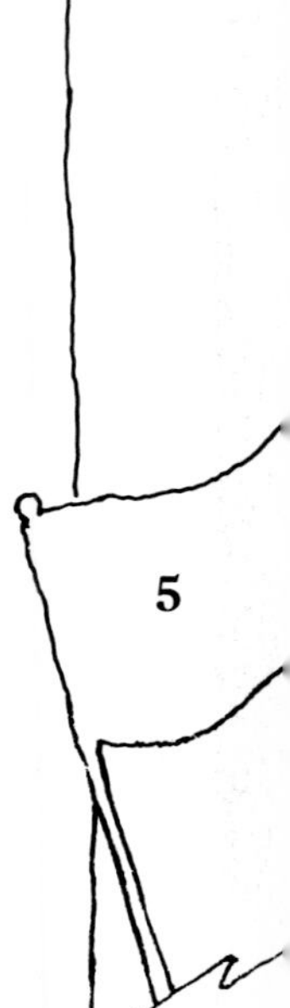
5

1. The earth orbits the sun at 18.5 miles per second (See April Fun Fact) **2.** An anteater can devour up to 30,000 ants in one day (See February Fun Fact) **3.** In Tunisia, it snows for the first time in 25 years (January 13) **4.** A man parachutes onto the World Trade Center in New York City (September 10) **5.** Greece becomes the 10th member of the European Common Market (January 1) **6.** A meteorite crashes into 13-year-old Anthony M. Sarkis, Jr.'s, backyard (October 31) **7.** The swallows return to San Juan Capistrano, California, from their winter stay in Argentina (March 19) **8.** Starfish have eyes on the ends of their arms (See June Fun Fact) **9.** Dolphins are being trained to help find sunken treasure (June 23) **10.** A fisherman spots the famous Lake Champlain sea monster (June 10) **11.** Four seals, suffering from hardware disease, are released from a zoo in Oregon (November 24) **12.** President Reagan gives the CIA permission to spy inside the U.S. (December 4) **13.** The take from a robbery in 1957 is discovered in Connecticut (See October) **14.** Happy 50th birthday to the Empire State Building (May 1) **15.** 2,500 guests attend the marriage of the Prince of Wales and Lady Diana Spencer (July 29)

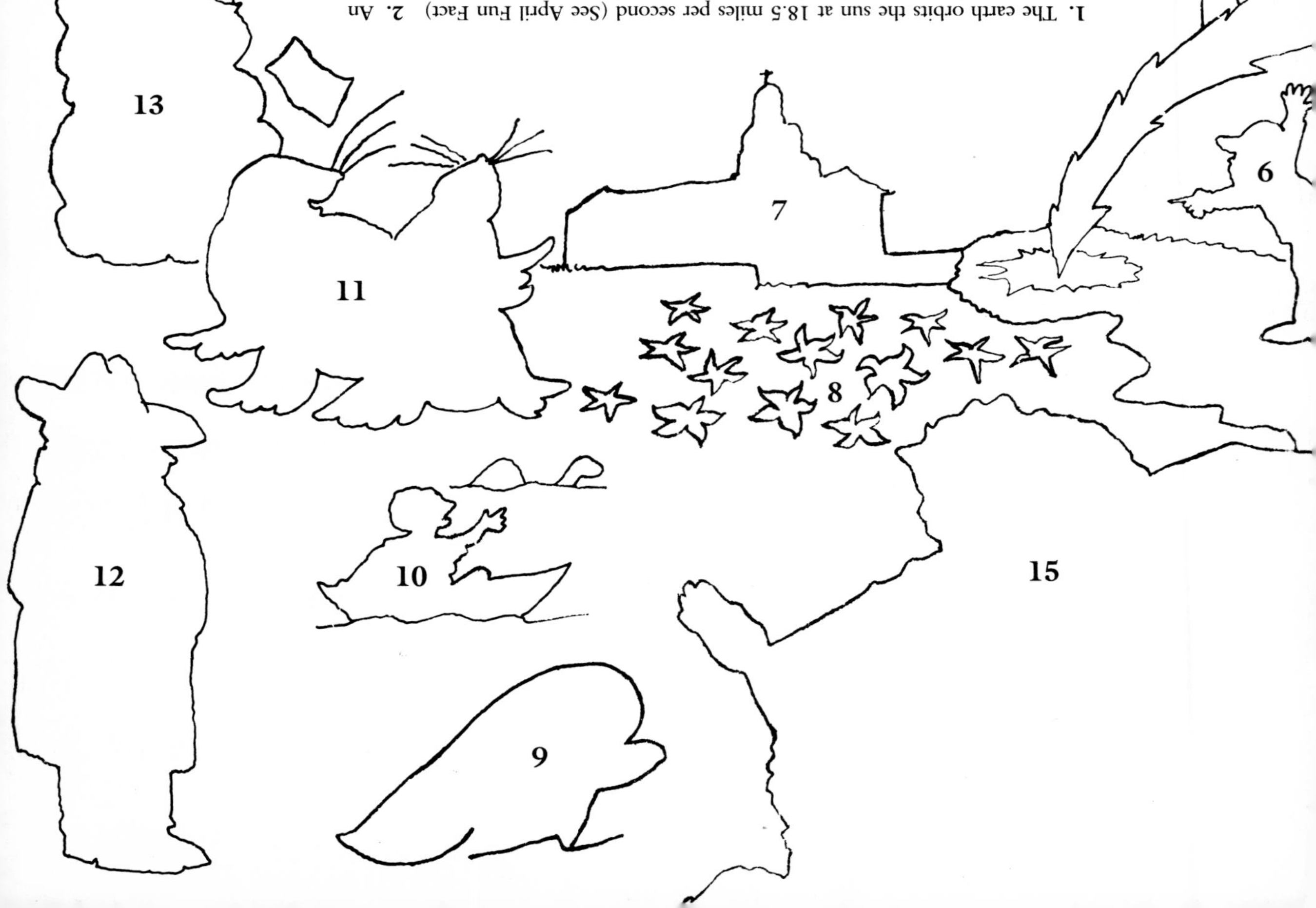
13
7
6
11
8
12
10
15
9